PRAISE FOR

Lewis Black and *Me of Little Faith*

"Lewis Black—the most engagingly pissed-off comedian ever."

—Stephen King

"About as funny as an altar boy's haircut. Which is to say—pretty hilarious."

—Bostonist.com

"Whenever I'm asked, 'Who makes you laugh?' or 'Who would you pay to see?' I don't hesitate for a moment. Lewis Black! Period. He's got it all: brains, balls, and chops."

—George Carlin

"While Lewis Black's second book, *Me of Little Faith,* is no doubt funny, the Comedy Central favorite and veteran comedian's collection of essays delve into highly philosophical territory, constantly exploring the author's spiritual evolution and ultimately creating something much more than a pile of slickly bound pages for your local bookstore's humor section. . . . While most comedy fans know Black as the volatile, always-agitated comic with a Joe Cocker–like delivery, *Me of Little Faith* exposes his softer side."

—*Punchline Magazine*

"Readers already familiar with Black will be pleased to find he rants just as well on the pages as he does in person. . . . Black's irreverence is laugh-out-loud funny."

—*Publishers Weekly* (starred review)

Most Riverhead Books are available at special quantity discounts for bulk purchases for sales promotions, premiums, fund-raising, or educational use. Special books, or book excerpts, can also be created to fit specific needs.

For details, write: Special Markets, The Berkley Publishing Group, 375 Hudson Street, New York, New York 10014.

ALSO BY LEWIS BLACK

Nothing's Sacred

me of little faith

LEWIS BLACK

EDITED BY HANK GALLO

riverhead books
new york

RIVERHEAD BOOKS
Published by the Penguin Group
Penguin Group (USA) Inc.
375 Hudson Street, New York, New York 10014, USA
Penguin Group (Canada), 90 Eglinton Avenue East, Suite 700, Toronto, Ontario M4P 2Y3, Canada
(a division of Pearson Penguin Canada Inc.)
Penguin Books Ltd., 80 Strand, London WC2R 0RL, England
Penguin Group Ireland, 25 St. Stephen's Green, Dublin 2, Ireland (a division of Penguin Books Ltd.)
Penguin Group (Australia), 250 Camberwell Road, Camberwell, Victoria 3124, Australia
(a division of Pearson Australia Group Pty. Ltd.)
Penguin Books India Pvt. Ltd., 11 Community Centre, Panchsheel Park, New Delhi—110 017, India
Penguin Group (NZ), 67 Apollo Drive, Rosedale, North Shore 0632, New Zealand
(a division of Pearson New Zealand Ltd.)
Penguin Books (South Africa) (Pty.) Ltd., 24 Sturdee Avenue, Rosebank, Johannesburg 2196,
South Africa

Penguin Books Ltd., Registered Offices: 80 Strand, London WC2R 0RL, England

The essay "Punk Creationism" first appeared in *The Mole.*
The Laundry Hour is reprinted with permission from Mark Linn-Baker, William Peters, and Paul Schierhorn.

Book design by Stephanie Huntwork

First Riverhead hardcover edition: June 2008
First Riverhead trade paperback edition: June 2009
Riverhead trade paperback ISBN: 978-1-59448-377-6

The Library of Congress has catalogued the Riverhead hardcover edition as follows:

Black, Lewis, date.
Me of little faith / Lewis Black ; edited by Hank Gallo.
p. cm.
ISBN 978-1-59448-994-5
1. Black, Lewis. 2. Religious biography. I. Gallo, Hank. II. Title.
BL73.B525A3 2008 2008006833
200.92—dc22
[B]

PRINTED IN THE UNITED STATES OF AMERICA

10 9 8 7 6 5 4 3 2

This book is dedicated to my parents, Sam and Jeannette Black. You can blame them. If you do, you will get a call from my mother.

Since this book was first published George Carlin died. I would also like to dedicate this book to his memory. He was a huge influence and help in my career. And the world is a less funny place without him.

And to all the others who watch over me.
Ron Black. Bill Foeller. Rusty Magee.
Laurie Beechman. Tommy Gardner.

CONTENTS

me of little faith

Just give me one thing
I can hold on to
To believe in this living
Is just a hard way to go.

—JOHN PRINE,

"Angel from Montgomery"

PREFACE

thou shalt have no other gods before me

(except the one you believe in . . .)

I can think of no better place to write a book about religion than this, my ancestral homeland, Chapel Hill, North Carolina, where I attended the University of North Carolina as an undergraduate. None of my ancestors actually came from here—they all came from Russia and later settled in New York—but I like to imagine that they're from this place. It's less depressing. "Russia" in the original Russian means "gathering of depressed people with a penchant for vodka as self-medication."

Several years ago I went to St. Petersburg, Russia, where some of my family was from, and I felt as if I didn't belong at all. It didn't look as if it had changed much since the early 1900s, when the pogroms there convinced my family to get the hell out. In these pogroms, organized gangs of Russians terrorized and killed more than a few Jews. My Aunt Sonia suffered six saber wounds during one of these attacks. Luckily, her sister, my grandmother, had come to America at the age of sixteen and made enough money to bring her here before a seventh saber wound could be delivered. I can't even imagine a time when people used sabers, let alone what would possess the Russians to go after my ancestors, who weren't what one would call practicing Jews.

As I wandered the streets of St. Petersburg, I felt not even one root. Actually, it was kind of a dump. An amazing dump, filled with some spectacular pieces of architecture, like the Hermitage, but everything looked in desperate need of repair and a paint job. It looked like it must have looked in a nineteenth-century painting that someone had soaked in water for weeks. I don't think it was a really smart move for the Russians to have driven out the Jews; they would have been a big help. They sure know their real estate. Lucky break for me, though—I was much happier in North Carolina than I would have been going to school in the Urals, or Vladivostok, or Shtuppengrad.

I felt absolutely at home in Chapel Hill from the moment I arrived from the suburbs of Washington, D.C., forty years ago. At the time it seemed strange that a Jew from up north would feel comfortable in the South, but Chapel Hill was a place where there were only a few folks left who thought the South had won the Civil War. It's one of the few spots on earth where I have felt comfortable in my own skin. I don't feel that way in many places—hence the very attractive series of twitches one sees in my stage act. Maybe it's because I lived in Chapel Hill in a past life and if I scout around long enough I'll see my ghost wandering around the campus. (Maybe even in a crinoline—Jesus, what if I was a woman in my past life?) It is the first place I discovered my own voice and was able to take my first baby steps toward becoming a writer—a playwright, no less.

So to tackle a subject as complicated as religion, which I have no expertise in, I figured I would return to the place where I first found the words to express my point of view.

And then, of course, there is the inspiration provided by the vision of all the young coeds of my alma mater who fill the sidewalks with their loveliness and who are enough to restore one's faith in a just and loving God. But I digress...and as I stare longingly, I can feel the flames of hell lapping at my nutsack.

So why am I writing a book on religion? I wish I could tell you that God had appeared to me and commanded that I reveal unto the peoples of the earth all of his mysteries and that I was the Antichrist. (Now that's a cash cow waiting to happen.) But the Antichrist wouldn't write a book. He'd have a reality show and all sorts of digital downloads and he'd leave mind-altering messages on cell phones.

Yet I noticed as I began to write that there has lately been a glut of books about religion. Atheists and true believers, critics of all stripes and defenders of the faith, they have destroyed hundreds of thousands of trees with their knowledge, research, opinions, and beliefs. (This is so typical of my life. I decide to write a book on religion and as soon as I sign the contract, the shelves overflow with new books on the subject from every imaginable point of view. And so, yet again is my belief in God undermined. WHAT BULLSHIT! I could see if I wrote a book on Iraq. We can't seem to get enough of those. It's like Chinese food. You can read all you want on the subject but within minutes of finishing a book you are hungry for more.)

I guess the flood of these theology books makes sense, with the excesses of violence committed in the name of God wherever you look and the obscene power of religion in politics, in our homes, and in our lives. Or maybe it's just the growing sense that the world might end at any moment, which seems to hang in the air around us, like a late-afternoon thundershower. I guess this has sent the keyboards atwittering. Then, of course, there is the constant flow of books in which authors talk about their conversions.

So what am I, Lewis Black, stand-up comic and me of little faith, doing putting my two cents in about religion?

Because I think it's taken too seriously, and anything that takes itself too seriously is open to ridicule.

What am I thinking? When you write about people's beliefs, you are asking for it. Every page here has the potential to offend someone, somewhere, in perpetuity, throughout the universe. That doesn't even count the critics who will say it wasn't funny enough. Or serious enough. Or spiritual enough.

Religion? Funny? You've got to be kidding. I am kidding, but it's not going to be seen that way by everyone, which is exactly why you've got to keep poking fun at it. After millennia of religion being used as a club, either to scare the shit out of children or to send them to war, someone's got to search for organized religion's funny bone.

To put it as simply as I can: This is a book about my relationship with religion, where my—dare I say it?—spiritual journey has taken me. From the religious dead ends I have wandered down to the pinpricks of light I have seen and barely understood, it's all here, in all its complicated and infuriating glory.

And all of this is just my opinion, the way I look at religion, what it's meant and not meant to me. And why it makes me laugh.

So if religion has taken over your life and you don't want to think about it or laugh about it because it will upset you, DON'T READ THE GODDAMN BOOK.

EVER.

AND EVER.

AMEN.

ONE MORE THING

a new preface to the paperback edition

What I learned when I wrote this book:

The secret of life? No.

The way to inner peace? No.

The ability to live entirely present in each and every single moment of time? No.

(And by the way, as hard as I try to do that, I don't think I ever will. I always find myself obsessed with something in my past, looking for a clue to why I ended up in the moment I am in, so I am not living in the moment. Or I am preparing myself for a future moment, so that I will be sure to be completely immersed in it when it finally arrives and so once again I am not, as they used to say, Being Here Now.)

What I learned during the writing of this book was that even though you wrote a hardcover book, when it is published in paperback, the publisher wants you to add extra material to it, even though you thought the book was already done.

"Really," I said. "You want more?"

"Yes, we want to give those who bought the hardback a reason to buy the paperback, and we want to give those who didn't buy the hardback the feeling that they were brilliant because they waited for the paperback, not because they were being tight with a buck."

And if there ever was a time to be tight with a buck, it's now.

So since I can't give you a revelation about spirituality that would lead you to unlock the doors of your perception—thereby expanding your comprehension of the universe to the point where you were a master of it, and through such a revelation the book would be purchased by millions and lead to a much-needed early retirement on my part—wouldn't it be better if I added a chapter about how to make big money in America's new foreclosure market? "Hey, you're helping these people out—and making a bundle to boot!" But what do I know? Like most good Americans, I just do what I'm told.

So here I am, trying to catch your attention, which is all over the place as you're bombarded with more information than you should have to deal with. For crying out loud, your cell phone gives you more information than you can handle on any given day. (I imagine there is more information on your cell phone today than there was in the entire world in the year 1714.) As a matter of fact, you might even be reading this *on* your cell phone, as my publisher tries to insinuate me into every waking moment of your life. The people there actually wanted me to go door to door, but because they've already paid me, I put my foot down on that nonsense. Now they want to make their money back. And who can blame them?

Hundreds of employees and their families are depending on you, and so are the tax bases of their communities and this great country of ours. If you're just reading this standing around the bookstore and don't buy this book, it will exacerbate an ever-increasing downward economic spiral, coupled with insane health care costs and a bankrupt mortgage industry. And if that weren't enough, the next thing you know, we'll be outsourcing the printing of this book to the Chinese, and the ink will be lead-based and people will end up with all sorts of strange neurological diseases. As a result, fewer books will be published, and fewer children will be drawn to the magic of the written word, and they'll end up spending their days blasting holes in whores and pimps in the latest video games, their values destroyed, their lives ruined.

I could go on and on as we head toward new economic disaster. So please, do all you can to avert another national catastrophe. Buy as many copies of this book as you can.

Oh, and for those of you who think it's easy to write an essay like this—or even a whole book of essays like this: Fuck you.

And I would like to say to those of you who are thinking of writing a book: Don't. Stop right now.

Unless of course you get great joy out of sitting at a desk

and staring into space wondering why you agreed to write a book and you haven't got one thought in your head except this recurring question, which has no answer, because that would mean you could *think*, and if you could think, there might be something on the page in front of you.

After a few days a paragraph appears on the blank page you have stared at and wondered, "Why is the sheet of paper eight and a half by eleven? Who decided on that? Why can't it be four by four so that this lonely paragraph would look like a lot more?" Eventually, the words begin to trickle into a stream, and if you're lucky, even a torrent. Your one thought is followed by other thoughts. The words begin to flow onto the page. Soon there are even pages—a stack of them, by God.

Suddenly you think, "I am a writer. I can do this. This isn't so hard." You start to feel good about yourself.

Then the moment of realization hits you. Someone is going to read this. Someone who isn't me. Someone who won't like my book as much as I do, because that someone isn't me and doesn't realize what an accomplishment this is, and how important what I have written is to the world and how by the mere presence of these, my words, this world will be a better place.

And why should anyone care? Is this book really that important in the scheme of things? What makes me think that anyone could give a tinker's damn for what my blood and sweat have poured onto the page? Who the hell do I think I am, writing a book? And remember, critics are going to read this book and criticize it because that's what a majority of them do, because they can't write a book. They are jealous. And they know from having read thousands and thousands of books just what a weird book I wrote. They show their disappointment and contempt in words that I have to look up in a dictionary. They spill out their disgust, and my own self-loathing rises as I race through the review, tears in my eyes.

So think about it before you sit down and start writing. Maybe there's something you could do around the house, like talking to your children, so that they will have the kind of self-esteem that will ensure that they will never have to write a book.

What's the worst thing about writing a book? Remember what it was like when you were a kid on Sunday late afternoon, just after a really great weekend, and you hadn't thought about school at all and just as the sun begins to fade into darkness you hear your mother say, "Did you do your homework?"

That's what every day is like until the book is written, and rewritten, and rewritten. You have homework every day. It never stops. It's always there.

It's like your mother's voice haunting you with the words, "You know if you do a little more, you'll get extra credit."

in the beginning

As I slowly reached consciousness, everything was a mystery waiting to be solved. Unfortunately for me, I wasn't much of a problem solver.

Who was this giant shoving a bottle in my mouth? Who was this other giant who wasn't around all the time but when he did show up would poke me? What were all these shapes and forms and sights and sounds? What the fuck was going on?

Even as a kid, a sense of unease pervaded my being. As I learned to differentiate between these gentle and somewhat nurturing giants and to say Momma and Poppa, much to the giants' amusement, and as the routine of my daily life took shape and began to give me a simple understanding of what was around me, I also felt as if I was floating in a wet tissue that might tear at any moment.

These are the vague flashes of my toddler years from an ever-dimming memory. (I don't know if I am imagining this or not. It's the way I remember it. Maybe my brain likes the sound of it. However, I distinctly remember reading the inspiring story *The Little Engine That Could*. It says as much as any self-help book ever written.)

There was no God there to comfort my fears, and that has always bothered me. If he was going to make himself known, one would think that this would be the perfect time to do it. While a little infant is shitting his diaper and wailing in the night, wouldn't it be nice if God could have provided a sense of peace? I mean, if he truly is everywhere, why the fuck not in my cradle? Would it have hurt? What's a few seconds from He Who Is Eternal?

So it turned out that the existence of God is something that I'd have to learn. And my first contact with the Lord Almighty came through the *Golden Book of Bible Tales*, read to me by my parents. The book of Bible tales featured all the big dramatic stories: David and Goliath, Samson, Noah, and Moses. God was a big character in all of them. He was always the go-to guy. I didn't know what these stories had to do with me, but they—and He—certainly grabbed my interest.

They were all stories from the Old Testament. There was a reason for that. I don't know when my parents told me that we were Jews. Maybe it was the first Chanukah, or when my mother took it upon herself to explain why I couldn't go in the public swimming pool with the other children. (Just kidding.) In truth, my parents weren't very religious—no surprise, really, considering neither were the families they came from. We would celebrate the big holidays, and that was about it. God wasn't really present in our daily lives. Lucky break for him, he wouldn't have liked my mother's food.

Still, God was mentioned enough that you knew he was around. Somewhere. And if not for me, then for somebody else.

By the time I was getting ready to graduate from high school in 1966, *Time* magazine, of all publications, caused me to reevaluate my tenuous belief system with one splashy and provocative headline. Written in large red block letters on a stark black background, a headline in the magazine posed the following question: IS GOD DEAD?

What the hell! The Yahweh I had been introduced to was supposed to be immortal.

But maybe the editors of *Time* were on to something. One must remember the times we were living in. In the late fifties and the early sixties, the country seemed to be living on the brink of nuclear holocaust. Those were simpler times, and America had only one real enemy, the Soviet Union. The Soviets had tons of nukes aimed at us and we had tons of nukes aimed at them. Many people in this country spent their weekends building and outfitting bomb shelters in their backyards just in case the Commies dropped the big one on us. In retrospect, it was more than a little ridiculous. (And it became the basis of one of my favorite movies, *Dr. Strangelove*.)

These were the conditions that led many to feel that God

must be dead. (Or maybe he just had a great sense of humor. Nothing creates great comedy like tension.) In the year leading up to the headline, we were inundated with even more bad news. The war in Vietnam was escalating with breathtaking speed, hellish images of civil rights workers being beaten in the South filled our TV screens, and the assassination of black activist Malcolm X, tragically and ironically, kicked off 1966's National Brotherhood Week.

With all of that going on, why not a dead God? In fact, a better headline might have been DID WE KILL GOD?

Let's face it, if God was, in fact, dead, he did not expire naturally. Just as Christians are told that Jesus died for their sins, God obviously suffered his fatal collapse under the weight of America's collective, misguided savagery.

Either way, I remember thinking at the time, even if I don't believe in him, a dead God isn't good news.

death is the ultimate game show

Why do we need religion at all? Wouldn't life work just as well if we kept ourselves higher than kites on an assortment of drugs, so we could maintain the moronically blissful grin one sees on so many born-again Christians?

It always seemed strange to me that people gave up drugs for religion just to get high on their newfound beliefs. So, other than for health issues and to hold down a job, why give up the drugs? If they are working, why give up a part of your weekend for religious services? Isn't that when people do drugs? (If you stay on them it seems you're just one step closer to the ultimate goal. And, lest you forget, that goal is to be a blissful moron.)

Or why don't we just choose to live without any morals at all so we can constantly satisfy the insatiable wants and needs that haunt us humans, thereby insulating ourselves from the fears that are at the underbelly of everyday life?

Now, if these seemed like excellent alternatives to religion, if you are ready to embrace either one of these ideas, then you need to put this book down right now and dial 911 and turn yourself in.

IMMEDIATELY.

These might be good ideas for fifteen minutes, like in a mindless sort of reverie before you take a nap, but not as a lifestyle choice. As much as you may want your neighbor's flatscreen or his wife in order to stave off whatever demons haunt you, the result would be a world filled with real demons. Not to mention the ensuing chaos, which would be intolerable.

One of religion's great contributions to civilization is that it gave us some rules to follow, which allow a bit of order to be maintained, and so we can feel that kind of glee that comes from breaking those rules every once in a while.

So if you come up with the rules, you've got to have somebody who makes sure that people obey them.

Enter God, stage right, left, and center.

Who better than a supreme being who, like Santa, "knows if you've been bad or good, so be good for goodness' sake"—or you'll be toast, you little shit, so sayeth the Lord.

What's at the root of all religions?

Death! Or, more precisely, the fear of death.

The fact of the matter is that whenever we face our own mortality, nine out of ten of us immediately promise God that we will do anything if he will just make sure that we don't die. Nobody wants to die because no one really knows where they will be going after the lights go out. Except of course for the public relations genius who came up with the concept that a suicide bomber would immediately go to heaven and meet up with seventy-two virgins. (Which would be impossible, I think, as I haven't met one on earth.) And as lousy as things may get here in this life, with war and disease and famine and cell phones that are either giving us brain tumors or rendering us sterile, while not delivering the proper coverage, somewhere is sure as shit better than nowhere.

Religion gives us a destination to head toward. It's the Orbitz of death, and if you are as good as good can be, then you get to end up in first class and you don't have to go through the security line. You won't even have to take your shoes off. You are given your own wings. You have become your own airline. And you spend your day flying around heaven, because you believed in God. He's the one who punched your ticket.

So what's heaven like? I always imagined it as the equivalent of being pushed around on one of those dolphin strollers at Disney World when you're three. Or it's where you see every asshole you ever dealt with in life get his comeuppance.

Or it's the place that when you get there, everything becomes clear and you are able to finally say, "Oh, I get it." It's where you view extraordinary vistas from mountaintops you didn't have to climb.

It's where you realize you didn't have to spend your life awash in guilt over all the actions you felt guilt about because it is now made quite clear to you that those are exactly the actions you should have taken, and the people you thought you'd hurt have actually grown because of you and they have become better people because of your idiocy and thoughtlessness.

It's a magnificent green meadow that almost hurts your eyes to look at but by doing so it keeps you so alert that you never wander outside each and every moment of each and every instant of an eternity that now feels as if it were only a moment. All to a sound track that reflects your every movement, so that it is all the sounds you know you have always wanted to hear. And everything tastes like the first ice cream you ever tasted. And you spend your days in such an exquisite sense of calm that so overwhelms your being that even I stop twitching.

Death is the abiding mystery that is the root of all religions, except Scientology, which doesn't count because I refuse to consider seriously anything that Tom Cruise believes in. What about the miracle of our daily existence? Isn't that what inspired the world's great religions as well? No. Life gets old very quickly, until of course they tell you your number is up, which is when you start paying attention to the precious miracle you are about to lose. Besides, you know you are here; the bigger question is where you are going after here. (Art Buchwald, one of America's greatest satirists, saw it a little differently. He checked himself into a hospice in early 2006, expecting to die. He had himself taken off dialysis, and then, miraculously, lived for another year. He said, "I have no idea where I'm going, but here's the real question: What am I doing here in the first place?")

It's death that opens the door to the idea of God. God gives people the comfort that they are actually going somewhere after this life. The idea of going nowhere should scare the shit out of any normal person, I would think. Unless of course your life is so miserable that nowhere seems like an improvement. And then there are the atheists and agnostics, who feel that the lights go out and that's that. I don't see any comfort in that.

I have a pretty good idea that when I am given the final countdown I will not go gentle into that good night. No matter how logical a mind one possesses, when faced with the concept of a black hole without end the synapses rev into overdrive, leaving logic in the dust.

Let's face it, we're talking fear here. Fear of the unknown and fear of a known that makes no real sense without some unifying principle that allows us to sleep at night. Organized religions organize themselves around that fear. Each claims to be the one true way to get to heaven. The ultimate fear, of course, is—which door is going to be the gateway to heaven? Door number one or door number two or door number three?

notes from the land of dreidels and hamantaschen

It's fortunate for me, as a comic and an author, that if you are born and raised Jewish, there is always more to say about it. A whole lot more. It's endless, in fact. One might say Judaism is not merely a religion but a perfect neurosis. It is, in short, without beginning or end. It just is.

At the risk of sounding like former president Clinton, the definition of "is" may be a little too narrow here. Because, much like a health club, Judaism offers three different memberships—Orthodox, Conservative, and Reform.

Orthodox is the strictest. Those people are not kidding around. They figure the Bible is the word of God and, as they see it, God means what he says, and so do they. And that's why the Orthodox Jews have a lot of rules. Among them: You can't work from Friday sundown to Saturday sundown. You can't drive during that time, either, so you've got to walk to temple. And you can't even turn on your own oven—which is why you hire a Christian to come over and light the fire under the brisket.

The rules don't end there. You say a prayer and light a candle. You say another prayer and cut the bread. Orthodox Jews really like to pray. And when they're done praying at home, they go to services to pray with others. And when they're at the temple, they strap on a leather device with small boxes that contain prayers, and place a prayer shawl over their shoulders. The women, however, sit in a different section from the men—in many cases, upstairs. And the men must always wear a yarmulke, or skullcap. It looks sort of like a diaphragm, only bigger. (The Conservative and Reform Jews also follow this practice, but only in the temple.) Orthodox women are spared the birth-control headgear, but if they're married, they're expected to cover their heads. (This custom, however, has begun to lose traction.)

The Orthodox also have very strict dietary laws. These alone would make it impossible for me to become an Orthodox Jew. Dairy and meat can't be eaten at the same time. I don't know why and I don't want to know why. If you're really curious, go find out for yourself. I think it has something to do with the "milk of the mother" and the "meat of the calf" never being mixed, and so that means all dairy and all meat must be eaten separately. Does that help? Yeah, I figured it would.

These laws mean you need two complete sets of dishes, cookware, silverware, et cetera, so that there is no fucking way that meat and milk can ever carry on together.

But here's the deal breaker as far as I'm concerned. You can't put cheese in your roast beef sandwich. For God's sake, I thought Atkins had a lot of rules. So call me a bad Jew, but

I'm not living without Monterey Jack with my roast beef. I will use Jewish rye, but that's the only concession I'm willing to make.

Still, it seems to me that if people follow all the rules to be an Orthodox Jew, they should get to go to heaven without question, even if they are pricks. Because if you can follow all those rules, chances are you are going to be a prick. If it's not one rule, it's another...

And then there are all those dishes to wash. Talk about irritating. (And it's not like the old days, when you could get the women to do all those dishes. They may sit in a separate part of the temple, but they are no longer in the back of the bus. They have lives to lead, too. A lot of dishes means a lot of negotiation.)

And if all that weren't enough, you cannot eat shellfish. Any shellfish. Clams, oysters, lobster, crab, crayfish, shrimp—in other words, anything that makes going to Cape Cod seem like a real holiday. This was originally a dietary law established because of health issues, since at the time shellfish were not considered to be good for your health. Those issues have been resolved, but that doesn't stop the Orthodox Jew from making it a sin to eat the world's preeminent butter delivery system. You can, however, mix fish and dairy, although I don't know why you'd want to. Tuna parmigiana, anyone?

Along the same lines, and for the same reasons, you can't eat pork. I don't quite grasp how dietary fascism gets you closer to God, but I know I would never have survived this life without barbecue—real barbecue, Porky-fucking-Pig barbecue. Apparently, the Orthodox Jews believe the stomach is the way to the Lord. I'm still combing my desk for *that* memo.

Finally, and not all Orthodox Jews practice this, but I'm told there are married couples who have sex through a sheet with a hole in it. I don't know the reason for this rule, but I do know that there is no reason for a rule like that. None. This is purely and simply madness. You have to be insane to follow a rule like that. You just can't worship a God who has a rule like that, unless you think it makes you a better person. But I'd rather be a less better person who has a lot more fun.

As you've no doubt concluded by now, there are just too many rules for me to ever be an Orthodox Jew. It would be easier for me to be a Mormon. I think they're crazy, too, but at least I could live with their diet.

Conservative Jews, on the other hand, drop some of the aspects of the tough-love God of the Orthodox—if not all of them. It actually depends on what temple you go to. Conservatives keep to a service mostly conducted in Hebrew, and some of them even keep a kosher diet. But they don't seem to get crazy about it. It seems as if they want to make it a little easier to live in contemporary society while keeping one foot in the Orthodox world, just to hedge their bets.

I was raised as a Reform Jew. My parents were not cut out

for anything else. Keep it short, keep it simple, and speak English, please, so I know what's going on. We are talking fireworks, no sheets, and the all-you-can-eat buffet—SHRIMP INCLUDED!

The Reform movement was the branch of Judaism looking to become a part of America's melting pot. I think this is what my parents wanted and why they named my brother Ronald Steven Black and me Lewis Niles Black. (So that I could hear on numerous occasions, "Really? You're Jewish?") They also left New York City to live in Maryland, because as much as they loved their families, they wanted a bit of distance from them. We were a part of the first wave of middle-class families to settle the suburbs. Our neighborhood was a white one, as most of the suburbs were in the fifties, as the black population was living in the cities, as they awaited their breakthrough to the middle class and the end of de facto segregation. Our neighborhood was filled with followers of all forms of Christianity and Judaism. There were no Muslims or Hindus or Buddhists. I doubt if anyone in the neighborhood had even heard of Zen. There were kids who went to Catholic schools. At the age of fourteen, one of the more normal kids in the neighborhood was sent away to a super-Catholic school to prepare him for the priesthood. It was like he'd been kidnapped by the Catholics. We never saw him again. In light of recent horror stories from the Church, I now wonder what fate befell him. I was also surrounded by Baptists, Methodists, Presbyterians,

Episcopalians, Unitarians, and Orthodox and Reform Jews. There were even a few of the Baha'i faith. And there were no fanatics in the mix: All of us kids got along and enjoyed hearing about how each of us didn't understand what our religions were up to or what we were going to church or temple for. (I mean, God was screwing up our weekends!)

I went to Sunday school, as opposed to Saturday school, which would have made more sense, but then I would have missed baseball practice. (Eventually I did have to go to Saturday school, which meant a demotion to a lesser baseball team, resulting in ruining any chance of my becoming the professional baseball player I was born to be.) I attended Hebrew school on Wednesdays, so I could be bar mitzvahed. And I had a huge Hebrew vocabulary, about fifty thousand words at one point, which would have been of some use to me if I were an Orthodox Jew. Or if I were surrounded by people who actually spoke the language. My grasp of the language slowly drifted into a few vague memories, such that I can still pronounce the words but haven't a clue what most of them mean. I still am able to read the major prayers and translate them, though. I probably should put that on my acting résumé, under "skills." Which might help when they finally do the remake of *The Ten Commandments*. I'm no Edward G. Robinson, but I still think I'd make a great Dathan.

It turns out that I was born the same year as Israel became a state. These were two events that occurred in the universe at the same time but had absolutely nothing to do with each other. And yet the Jewish community and my temple tried to attach a huge significance to this coincidence. That somehow we were tied together in a deeply profound and mystical way. The State of Israel even invited all of us, every thirteen-year-old Jew in the D.C. area, to a big celebration of our collective bar mitzvah. I could understand it. Israel was a baby state surrounded by enemies; there were then no peace treaties between Israel and any of the Arab states. Its survival was extremely precarious—even more so than now, with Bush the Younger mucking the waters. It was as if an Arab–Israeli war could break out at any minute of any day. So why wouldn't Israel want to make a young Jew feel as if its survival was imperative and of vital importance to him? I had already been indoctrinated. What if there was another Hitler? Where could my people go? This was a part of my religious education, and every Sunday for years I brought my quarters to the temple to help buy trees to be planted in Israel. I never saw any pictures of trees, so maybe, in retrospect, I was helping chip in for a fighter plane or a bazooka.

I understood it, but it didn't work for me. As much as I wanted the State of Israel to survive, I didn't want to be a part of the State of Israel. All of the attempts they made to try and get me to feel a deep identification with Israel fell on ears that went from deaf to deafer. Hell, I just wanted to play ball.

I don't think it helped that my grandfather as a young

man had gone to Israel when it was still Palestine, early in the twentieth century. It wasn't even a country at that point. It was a protectorate. He didn't last long there—didn't like it there at all. His memories about it no doubt influenced my feelings. But more than that, it was when I read Kurt Vonnegut's *Cat's Cradle* that I really understood my feelings about Israel. It's there that I read about granfalloons and other false groupings. I felt like a Jew, I was a Jew, but I was not, by any stretch of the imagination, an Israeli. Sure we shared a bar mitzvah, sure it was where my religion was born, but, like it or not, it was not my country. This also probably affected my feelings about being a Jew. I wasn't going to let them sucker me. I'm a Jew. I'm not stupid.

One of the good things about a bar mitzvah is it is a solid background for when you have to get up in front of a class and speak to the room. After winging it and singing along in Hebrew in front of your family and friends, "What I Did Last Summer" was a breeze. It also gave me my first joke as a stand-up. To wit:

"I broke into show business when I was very young. I was bar mitzvahed. That's a gig we Jews have, say a few prayers over a credit card and, BAM, you're a man. It marks the passage to puberty, but not its cure. There is no book of the Bible that deals with puberty. I made $1,200 that day and a set of golf clubs. That would be worth about ten grand today. When my dad saw the cash flow in, he quit his job and we moved from town to village where Jews dwelled and we would put on another bar mitzvah."

It didn't kill, but it at least sounded like a joke. It was a start.

While my bar mitzvah was a simple catered affair, bar mitzvahs today are completely out of control. Money is no object. Hundreds of thousands of dollars can be spent on the food, the hired entertainment, and the themes or locations. It can be an all-day affair that takes place at some exotic location and can stretch from breakfast through dinner, where a major rock-and-roll star can perform. Sometimes the guests are flown to another state, or even country. Religious events become a spectacle the ancient Romans would drool over. These days enough is never enough—enough is what the neighbors do. It's like a Jewish Cirque du Soleil, but with more noshes.

Even more insane than the bar mitzvah can be, a bark mitzvah was held in New York City at the Boathouse in Central Park. My psychiatrist, Martha, heard about it from a friend who went to it. She and her dog, that is. That's right—a bar mitzvah was held for a dog, and people attended and brought their dogs. I wish Martha had gone so I could tell you more. But just let your imagination run wild—it probably doesn't even come close to what went on there.

How does someone have a bar mitzvah for a dog and not end up committed? Couldn't a psychiatrist have taken out papers on this lady, just for her own good? And how did her dog not turn on her and maul her? My bar mitzvah probably didn't hold a candle to the treatment that dog got.

I have to say that my education in the Jewish religion was excellent. It was thorough, both from historic and biblical standpoints. So when, at the age of fifteen, I was confirmed and made my choice about practicing the faith of my fathers, it was based on knowledge. Maybe they shouldn't have taught me so well, because it probably led to too much thinking.

One of the papers I wrote for my confirmation class (yes, we had to write papers) was a real eye-opener. I discovered a story about a very wealthy and deeply religious man. He wondered if it made a real difference whether one followed a spiritual path or a path of dissoluteness—in other words, if one chose to be a saint or a sinner. So he quit his upright life and went down the road of sin. He broke one biblical law after another. He consorted with hookers and criminals.

And what did he discover?

THAT IT MADE NO DIFFERENCE IN HIS LIFE. NONE.

He didn't feel guilty. The Lord didn't punish him for his sins. He concluded that both roads led to the same place.

Wow. Even today, that's all I can say to that. You've got to admire a religion that would let that story out, especially to kids. But it sure made me think about whether I wanted to lead an upright life as a Jew or, well, live the life I've been living. I obviously chose the latter, so pass the martini and suck my dick.

One of the good things about my Sunday school classes was that they gave me a lesson in comparative religion. They sent me to a variety of other houses of worship—Catholic, Lutheran, Episcopalian, Baptist, Islamic, Baha'i, Buddhist, and who knows where else. It was a spiritual smorgasbord. It was excellent, because I realized it wasn't just my own temple that didn't appeal to me. None of the others did, either.

There was something about organized religion that just didn't do the trick for me. Sitting with a bunch of people at a religious service, any religious service, anywhere, has never brought me closer to God. I don't know what it is. It seems to work for tons of people, and it makes them really happy, but for me it all gets lost in the translation. Maybe it's the sarcastic prick in the dunce cap who sits in my head and has a comment about everyone and everything that's going on. All I know is that by the time I was fifteen and my religious education at the temple was over, I was over Judaism. I have rarely looked back to the fold. When I have, it has just reinforced my initial impulses.

In the mid-1970s, when I was at the Yale School of Drama, my friend Tommy Gardner proposed that we go to the Yom Kippur service at a temple just down the road from the suburb of New Haven where a number of my fellow drama school students and I were sharing a house. I have never been a big fan of the Yom Kippur service. Also known as the Day of Atonement, Yom Kippur is the day God writes your name in the Book of Life or the Book of Death.

Yep, God apparently does all of his own bookkeeping, and all in one day. Talk about a strict deadline. What if he makes a mistake? I've been audited—I know these things can happen.

As a result, Yom Kippur gives me the creeps. But I was older then and more mature. I was in grad school. I thought, Let's give it another chance. Maybe God would finally reveal himself to me. Maybe there would be some hot single girls there. Or maybe none of the above.

Anyway, my little field trip with Tommy Gardner brought it all back. The spooky strains of the Kol Nidre, the sense of foreboding that God was getting out his pen to write my name in the Book of Death, and just sitting with all those people. Making matters worse, the rabbi used his sermon to appeal to us to buy State of Israel bonds. I shit you not—he used Yom Kippur as a backdrop to a money pitch for war bonds. "Oh, heavenly father, I beseech you, what is wrong with my peeps?"

Since that day, I have only entered a temple in order to perform. For reasons that escape me I have been asked to perform in a few temples, but have only done it once. Yep, they have to pay me to go into the house of the Lord.

I also never have found any of our holidays to be a big draw. Now, Passover is really quite beautiful, I will admit, in its commemoration of our leaving Egypt and crossing the desert, as the comedian Ron Zimmerman once said long ago, in order to be free to settle in Miami Beach. Christianity has nothing like it.

What spoiled Passover for me was a visit my family made when I was twelve to see my grandmother and her third husband at a hotel near Spring Valley, New York, to celebrate the holiday with them. There were hundreds of people at a huge catered seder (the ritual meal of Passover). It was my step-step-grandfather's last supper, so to speak, as it was clear at that point that he was dying. There were many elderly people in attendance. It was an Orthodox rabbi who led us through the meal, in Hebrew, but you could hardly hear him for the chaos in the room. It was like a Sunday brunch at a Hyatt. Kids running amok and parents alternately screaming at their offspring to behave better and at their waiter to serve better. It was appalling. I may not believe, but I believe if you are in the presence of believers, you should show a little respect for their beliefs.

As much as I don't like rituals, I do respect them, and I understand the need for them. I just don't get much from them. But to watch these old men try to pray and get us through the seder while all hell was breaking loose around them was more than disturbing. Those old men deserved better than that. They deserved some respect for their beliefs, even if you didn't get your food on time.

That's what killed Passover for me. That and the brisket that my mother would cook for every Passover meal, a brisket boiled to the point that it looked and tasted like a thousand rubber bands.

Then there is Purim, which you can read about in the Book of Esther, if you are so inclined. This is a holy day because a plot by Haman, a Persian nobleman, to annihilate all the Jews in Persia was thwarted. And how do we celebrate this special day? By eating a pastry called hamantasch, which is apparently in the shape of Haman's hat. The hamantasch is a prune pastry, by the way, and only we Jews would think to celebrate our survival by scarfing down a natural laxative. I realize I am nit-picking, but it all adds up in the end.

The real deal breaker for me, though, was Chanukah. Or, as they still pronounce it in many places, Haanuuukaaaah. Which is not to be confused with how they pronounce it in the Deep South, which is Cha-*Noo*-Kah. None of these pronunciations is correct, however. Actually, in Hebrew it is pronounced with all the phlegm that one can summon, so that the "Ch" has a real *hock* sound to it. (Hebrew, incidentally, is truly a language of phlegm. That's because we were in the desert for so long. If you didn't keep the phlegm going, you were never going to make it to the next watering hole.)

For reasons that will always remain a mystery to me, we celebrate Chanukah during the same month as Christians celebrate Christmas. When you compare these two holidays, there is only one conclusion: Christmas is great and Chanukah sucks. Next to Christmas, Chanukah looks like a retarded crafts fair.

To begin with, Christmas is celebrated with electricity.

There are lights everywhere: on the streets, on the tree, on the house—everywhere, for Christ's sake. And what are the lights saying? They're saying, "We're having fun! We're having fun! And you're not, 'cause you're a Jeeeew!"

We celebrate Chanukah with candles. Itty-bitty, shitty candles, as if we are living in a cave in the fifth century and hydroelectric power is unknown to us. We are supposed to light the candles for eight days, but most Jewish families are lucky if they make it to day five.

"Gee, Pop, aren't we going to light the candles tonight?"

"Awwwww, fuck it. We ran out of candles. It's the same thing as last night, only one more candle. You remember last night, don't you? Do we really have to keep this up? For God's sake, stop crying! You want to see a light, I'll open the oven and we'll look at the pilot light."

On the first night of Chanukah, Jewish families do something that can only be described as sadistic. They give their children a top to play with. That's right, A TOP! A TOP! They call it a dreidel, but I know a top when I see one. You can call it the king's nuts if you want, it's still a top.

For God's sake, a top is not a toy. A toy is something you play with. You stare at a top. All a top is good for is if you have toddlers and want to see how they are going to do in school. Just spin a top in front of them. If they stare at it for more than fifteen seconds, you are fucked.

A top is like giving a young girl who expects a Barbie doll

a stick and telling her to give it a name. What do you do with a top? You spin it. That's all you can fucking do with it. Spin it. "Oh boy, look at that, someone get me an asthma inhaler. I can barely breathe I'm having so much fun. And tell me, what are we going to do now? Spin it again?"

Not on my watch.

I used to take the top and shove it up my ass. It was no fun up there, but it was a whole lot better than playing with it. My parents used to come in and ask where the dreidel was and I'd say I didn't know. And then I'd plead, "For God's sake, don't buy another." All a top taught me was that I had better find another religion, one that knew what a good time was all about.

On Christmas Day, I would go to my Christian pals' houses to see what they got. Sure enough, they got everything that I had wished for. Everything. They even got really great stuff I hadn't even thought of. And that was where I learned what the word "covet" meant. It was as if Santa was taunting me. "See what I do for the Christians, Jewboy?"

Afterward, I'd go home and see what I got that night for Chanukah. That's when I first learned what depression was. I got a pen-and-pencil set.

"Really, a pen-and-pencil set! I am so glad I have two eyes, one for each eye. Oh, how did you get the name of the bank off the marble base?"

And the fun didn't stop there. The second night I received

a notebook. How do you play with a notebook? Put your penis between the two flaps and whack it. That's a short game.

The next night was even better. I got socks. SOCKS! There's a real showstopper. "Hey, WHY DON'T YOU GIVE ME SOME BUTTONS TO SEW ON THEM SO I CAN MAKE SOME SOCK PUPPETS. AT LEAST THEN I WOULD HAVE SOMEONE INTELLIGENT TO TALK TO. THIS IS SUPPOSED TO BE A FUN HOLIDAY GIFT, NOT A CARE PACKAGE."

The fourth night I got an eraser, which was good, 'cause it helped get the top out of my ass.

By the fifth night, I just stopped asking, I couldn't handle any more disappointment.

Now, don't get me wrong, none of this means that I now celebrate Christmas. Over the years, I have gone with girlfriends to their homes for Christmas and have watched their families melt down at the dinner table. It never made for a good meal. Let's face it, icy stares across the table and blame being spit back and forth at ear-shattering decibel levels aren't the path to good digestion. Even for you Catholics and WASPs.

I do believe, however, that food is as important as religion. And I don't think it's right for families to be screaming at each other on Christmas Day. After all, you don't want to wake the baby Jesus, do you?

So as a result of all this—and more that I absolutely refuse to dredge up from memory—I have left the fold. I still call myself a Jew, even though I don't practice the faith. And I don't buy that I am what some people refer to as "a cultural Jew." That just sounds like a weird kind of yogurt.

I may not practice the faith, but it's still there, way down deep in the caverns of my brain. And there is no denying that my DNA is awash in Jewishness. Otherwise, why would I feel so guilty about writing this chapter?

getting in touch with god

How do we contact God?

After all these millennia, have we finally gotten smarter about reaching him? Has he? Does he have a switchboard? I mean, with billions of people of all religions trying to make contact, how does he work it?

"Good afternoon, Judaism, may I help you? Please hold, Islam's on line two."

Then again, maybe heaven has gone automated and like everybody else is using IT guys in Bangalore.

"You have reached the Highest Consciousness / The Mind of God. *Para continuar en español, marque dos ahora*. If you know your party's extension, you may press it at any time. For the Almighty, press one. For Vishnu, press two. For the Holy Ghost, press three. For Yahweh, press four. To hear these choices again, press zero."

While it's true that many of these religions think they are the only true religion, the one true way to God and eternal salvation, this is all—and I'm going to burst a bubble here—absolute bullshit. How do I, the least religious person on the planet, know this? Because that attitude is the spiritual equivalent of having a favorite team you root for. (However, the Duke-Carolina rivalry borders on being a holy war, but that's a whole other story.) Because what's true for you may not be true for the guy standing next to you. We all work differently. Each of us is full of shit in our own special way. We are all shitty little snowflakes dancing in the universe.

Besides, this is God we're talking about, not the Dallas Cowboys, and you just can't claim ownership of God. If you think you can, you're an idiot. He's not property—and if he is, then he has been illegally subdivided. Religious rule of thumb: You do not possess God. God owns your tired ass.

In fact, you can't even *lease* God—although plenty of people have tried over the course of civilization. How many mass murderers have made that last, lonely walk to the electric chair clutching a Bible? As if God were going to forgive their previous sins because they could now quote Deuteronomy. Call me a skeptic, but I know hell was invented for a reason, and it wasn't to allow leaders who go to war to think that that's where their enemy will end up.

So if God does exist, he does not come with a damage deposit.

There is no more egregious example of this than on the courts and playing fields of organized athletics. There is nothing more obnoxious to an avid sports fan—okay, to me—than an athlete telling the audience after a big victory that God was the reason for it. As Jeff Stilson puts it so well in his act: "I like football games, but I hate the interviews after the games, because the winning players always give credit to God while the losers blame themselves. Just once I'd like to hear a player say, 'Yeah, we were in the game... until Jesus made me fumble. He hates our team. Jesus hates us.'" It implies that the losers on the other team just didn't love God enough or have enough faith in the Supreme Being.

I can't believe—in fact, I don't believe—that God likes that. He's got to be wondering what kind of egos these overpaid blowhards—many of them 'roided to the teats—have if they honestly think that He, with all that is going on throughout the universe, is worried about a stupid game and whether one wife-beating schmuck or another is going to win it. So many of these athletes go on and on with "Jesus this" and "Jesus that," they sound more like bad prophets than pro athletes.

And so it was written in the Book of Shaq: "'Oh boy,' God exclaimed on the twelve trillionth day, 'I have to get my boy into the NBA finals.'"

These athletes always give the same speech, and it goes something like this:

"First I have to thank my Lord and Savior, Jesus Christ. He is the one who brought me here to this victorious moment. It is through his love and the promise of eternal salvation that I was able to achieve this triumph. I cannot even begin to tell you how many times I wanted to just give it up, and Christ just lifted me up out of my miserable wretchedness so that I could slam-dunk a basket. I love Jesus and if he were here right now I'd be gaga gay for him."

Okay, so maybe I'm paraphrasing here, but you get the idea. The guy is thankful, but get a grip. God just doesn't have time to keep score.

knock, knock. who's there?

> "How do you know you're God?"
> "When I pray to him I find I am talking to myself."
> —FROM *THE RULING CLASS* BY PETER BARNES

When I began to think about God, I was scared to death of Him from the very beginning. I got absolutely no comfort from him, no joy, no sense of solace that he would shelter me from my myriad fears. In Judaism, God isn't a touchy-feely, smiley kind of a guy. He's Yahweh, and he's miserable and reminds me a lot of my ninth-grade lab science teacher. He never smiled. He barely opened his mouth and his lectures were inaudible. And once he gave you a grade, that was it. You couldn't argue with him about it, even if you were right.

If my lab science teacher scared the shit out of me, imagine what God was doing to my frail psyche. Since my biggest fear was, in fact, God himself, I was pretty much fucked in the whole spiritual arena from the get-go. That is the biggest reason why I have never been able to believe in any formal religion, or, for that matter, in even a casual one. Which explains why I have never been very good with prayer.

From the very start I was just too self-conscious for the whole exercise. Whenever I was told by the rabbi to bow my head in prayer, I felt like an abject failure because the only voice I would hear would be my own.

I had no real idea to whom I was speaking. Or even if anyone was actually listening. I figured that God might be eavesdropping, but I could never be sure. And if everyone else around me at temple was praying at the same time, I would wonder which one of us he was listening to. And how was he grading our prayers? Was he looking for sincerity, need, uniqueness, or just something to humor him?

My brain would be abuzz with these kinds of questions—which caused such static in my head that my meager and rather self-serving prayers would get lost in all of the noise.

All of this gave way to a much more disturbing question: How happy is God going to be with me if I am questioning the only means of communicating to him available to me? Try as I might, I never did locate that Lewis-to-God telex office. I have never been able to just let go and feel like I am really talking to God.

Unless, of course, you count those times when something horrible happens.

Such as when the doctor used the words "unspecified infection." Or when I was looking out the airplane window and oil from one of the engines splattered all over it and the captain instantly came on and said we were going to land immediately. Or during a six-hour IRS audit.

In those moments when I actually prayed I always felt disingenuous, as if I were saying the lines of a character that I didn't understand. So I prayed with some trepidation, figuring that it had to be some sort of sin to dial up God only in case of emergencies—usually emergencies I could have prevented by wearing a condom or having someone do my taxes who spoke English.

Perhaps I am not much of a transmitter. Maybe there's a class I could take for that.

jesus loves me, this i know

Well, I don't know. As I think I've made clear by now, I don't believe in Jesus. For crying out loud, my parents didn't allow a Christmas tree in the house. I mean, you just can't be Jewish and believe that Jesus is the son of God. It's the deal breaker.

What about Jews for Jesus? you ask. To put it simply, I think they're nuts. It sounds like they are going to *vote* for the guy. For centuries, being a Jew was tough enough. What makes you think Jesus is going to help? He's one of the major reasons it was hard to be Jewish. It took years for the Christian community to get over the fact that we probably had him whacked. Mel Gibson still carries a grudge. For God's sake, it's the reason he had a drinking problem. Or as he liked to put it, "For the love of Christ, get me a margarita."

I have to say that I was disappointed when the Catholic Church let the Jews off the hook. For centuries they were absolutely sure that we were intimately involved in the crucifixion of Jesus, even the Jews born hundreds of years after the deed was done.

I have never felt the need to be macho because I knew that my people had killed God's only begotten son, and that was all I needed on my résumé. Christ-killer sure beats being called a kike. Of course, either expletive is usually followed by a good ass kicking. But I felt it kind of gave me a leg up. "I killed your savior, so bring it on." Talk about the ultimate fighting match.

And why were Catholics so pissed at us? If someone didn't kill Jesus, there'd be no Christianity. (Much like if Anna Nicole Smith hadn't died, she wouldn't be famous.)

But I have to admit, I love the *concept* of Jesus. Once you have Judaism, with all of its rules, then it makes sense that a guy like Jesus—who was himself a Jew—comes along and says, "Okay, God gave us the rules we are supposed to follow, so here's what I am going to do. I am actually going to follow them to the letter of the law." What then? You got the beginning of Christianity is what you got. Practice what you preach if you will. (Without Judaism, there is no Christianity—much like, on the earthly level of political stupidity, if there is no Bill Clinton, there is no George W. Bush. It takes a minor idiot to show us what a real idiot is. Then again, if everyone was Christlike, there would be no need for politicians at all.)

It's logical to me that there was once someone like Jesus. I just find it hard to believe he is the son of God. God seems to me to be above the whole family thing. If God is all-seeing and all-knowing, then I think he'd have the common sense not to get involved with that kind of potential mess. When you've got universes to deal with, who's got time for a kid? Besides, if he had a son, even though he could be a prick at times, I don't think he's going to let him get crucified. It sure is a lousy precedent to set.

And the Lord said: "Always keep a large wooden cross handy around the house. Just in case any of your kids screw up, I'll crucify them."

the yoshimura code

During my first year at the Yale School of Drama—yes, I have a master's in fine arts from an Ivy League institution, there is a God—my friend Jim Yoshimura, a fellow student in my class of playwrights, and I would have extended arguments about Catholicism and Judaism. As I remember them, I argued the fallacies I saw in Jim's Catholic religion and he would defend them while going after the inconsistencies he found in Judaism. (As you can see, we had a lot of time on our hands, and we needed to fill it with whatever we could grab on to, as the schooling was costing us both a small fortune and we didn't want to think about that for one second longer than we had to. How were we going to pay for this? We were going to be playwrights, for crying out loud. We might as well have majored in professional begging.)

Don't get me wrong—I really like Catholicism. It appeals to my sense of theater. You gotta love the pomp and the incense and the chanting and the costumes, and when the Mass was said in Latin, I was absolutely enthralled. It was a hell of a lot better than *Cats* and most of the experimental theater I saw during that period. And they even served wine and hors d'oeuvres.

As impressed as I was with the Mass, there are way too many downsides to Catholicism for me to convert anytime soon. (I did once make the offer to convert for cash. The good people at Villanova University offered me an awful lot of money to perform for the student body there, with the stipulation that I did not make fun of the Catholic Church. I told them for an extra ten grand I would start by accepting the infallibility of the pope and anything else they wanted. They declined.)

For starters, the history of the Catholic Church is littered with more bullshit than I can put up with. Remember the "indulgences," where a little money went to making sure that your sins were forgiven? Or how about the Crusades, where hordes of really pissed-off Europeans trample the Holy Land to free it from the infidels? And then there's the Inquisition, which yanked the faithful back into the fold kicking and screaming (and threw in a little maiming to make things interesting). Call me a pussy, but these things don't sit well with me.

But Jim had no problem defending the Church. And he had no problem with the idea of a pope. I, on the other hand, have always thought it made no sense. It wasn't logical to me that one guy would be chosen to be *the* guy to get all the communication from God. I don't trust the whole notion of it.

The pope is like God's cell phone to the rest of us. As holy as someone can be—and even I have to admit that there have been some very holy men as popes—it's still tough for me to trust that their human brains and their prejudices don't get in the way of the messages from the big guy himself. Especially since they're celibate. (That's a lonely road I don't think anyone should go down. Trust me, I have been from time to time—not by choice, mind you—and I believe it causes semen to back up, which isn't good for either the heart or the mind. And you don't want to be around me when I haven't had sex in a while. It's ugly. Very ugly. Hey, I'm no walk in the park when I'm getting some, so you can only imagine.)

Think about it. The history of the papacy is littered with felonious popes. (That would be a great name for a band, by the way. I would definitely buy a Felonious Popes CD.) And it's not as if God comes down here every time and says on *Larry King*, "Hey, I've chosen the next pope." It's all political.

The pope is selected by a vote in the College of Cardinals that has to convene in the Sistine Chapel at the Vatican and stick around until a majority of them vote for one of the guys in the room. That can take days, or weeks, or even months. If we picked a president that way, it would kill anyone trying to run. (If that weren't enough, it's another all-boys club doing the voting. Can you believe that no women help make such a monumental decision? Has anyone in the Vatican looked at a clock in...forever? Do they know what century this is? What are the nuns for, decoration? Well, if so, I say you should look for some hotter uniforms. And by the way, the Catholic schoolgirl's uniform is the most haunting of all fantasywear I have come across in my lifetime. But I fear I share too much...)

I am definitely in favor of a pope God himself chooses.

So what did my friend Jim have to say to all this? Why could he believe Catholic doctrine, even though he rarely—if ever—attended church?

He had faith, he told me.

Faith.

And that was the key to all of my confusion. It's just a matter of faith. Faith that the pope is celibate and is *fine* with it, and he's handing down dictums to be followed by people who aren't.

And Jim's not alone. There's a trickle-down theory at work in the church. The celibate priest advises married couples, and the celibate nun advises teens on their sexuality.

All I need is faith, Jimmy?

Faith in what? Faith in the fact that I can suspend the human thought process in order to allow this kind of lunacy?

"No," Jim would say. "It's the faith that brings sanity."

And here's the best part: He would tell me the pope is infallible.

How do you know that, Jimmy?

"Faith, you ninny."

I have to admit that faith is extremely powerful. When I looked at Jim, who's a smart guy, he seemed to accept the fact that the pope knows what he's talking about, that the Church, despite its history of being greedy and violent and underhanded and a home for sexual predators, does want to help people be better. It makes you wonder if Jimmy is on to something: It's been working for a lot of people for a long, long time.

I suppose it all depends on where you want to plug your life into. It's like choosing between AOL and Google.

If you have the faith to believe in the absolute truth of the Catholic Church and its teachings, then there is no need for questions. You are set. You don't need to worry about a spiritual mortgage, wondering if you can make each payment. You've already bought the farm. You are set.

If you believe the pope is infallible and all he says is true, then you are relieved of the responsibility to think about what he tells you that you should believe. It's a marvelous system that helps bypass logic. It's what makes all religions tick.

My understanding of Judaism, for example, is that by practicing on a daily basis in prayer and thought and deed, you need not question a God who is making your way for you. And then there's the born-again Christian, whose faith can move mountains, perform daily miracles, and leave the believers safe in the knowledge that everything happens for a really good reason.

And you don't have to take that on faith. You can take it from me. I know about these things.

Really. I prayed about it.

the cathojewlic

I have never understood converting from Judaism to Catholicism. Or, for that matter, converting the other way.

To begin with, both religions are squarely rooted in guilt. And while each faith deals with guilt very differently, neither does a good job of coping with it. So why switch from one to the other?

At least that's what I thought until I read about the French cardinal Jean-Marie Lustiger, who passed away in 2007. Born a Jew in Paris in 1926, Lustiger was sent by his parents to Orléans to live with a Catholic woman after Paris fell to the Nazis at the beginning of World War II. At the age of thirteen—ironically, when he should have been bar mitzvahed—Lustiger decided to convert to Catholicism. His parents, to say the least, weren't pleased. Apparently, they did not see the humor in it. (In a very sad twist, his mother died at Auschwitz.)

After taking a degree at the Sorbonne, Lustiger studied for the priesthood and was ordained in 1954. He rose through the ranks of the Catholic Church and eventually became bishop of Orleans and, later, the archbishop of Paris. At one point he started to learn Hebrew and thought about emigrating to Israel. He wasn't so much marching to the beat of a different drummer as marching to the beat of a drummer with two separate drum kits.

"I was born Jewish," he said once, "and so I remain, even if that is unacceptable to many. For me the vocation of Israel is bringing light to the Goyim [non-Jews]. That is my hope, and I believe that Christianity is the means for achieving it."

This may have been the ultimate Underground Railroad approach. But you have got to admire the balls on this guy. He proclaimed his Jewishness until his death. Which didn't seem to bother the Catholics as much as it did the Jews, WHO NEVER GRASPED LUSTIGER'S IDEAS ABOUT KNOWING GOD. He was even considered as a possible successor to Pope John Paul II.

Could you imagine that? A converted Jew becomes pope. Oh, the damage we could have done.

As it turns out, we didn't need to get one of ours into the Vatican's top spot to screw things up. The Catholic Church has been managing to do it very well all on its own.

the rapture

If Jesus returns to earth, as many Christians believe he will, how will we know it?

In the midst of an information explosion and with a multitude of idiots with nothing to say clogging our airwaves, how would he manage to get even a few minutes of our attention? God help him if he doesn't hire a really good publicist. Trust me, he's dead meat without a real shark in his corner.

Considering the sea of hairless hoo-hahs and perfect tatas exposed by the drug-addled young starlets who are grabbing all of the headlines, Jesus certainly has his work cut out for him. He might even have to get the attention he is looking for by immediately going into rehab. He could say that returning was a real shock to his system and so he started self-medicating on various painkillers and cheap red wine. Even if he does manage to grab a smidgen of our attention from online porn, eBay, YouTube, Facebook, MySpace, and the whole hysterical cyberspace of bloggers, who among us is going to take seriously someone who looks like any other Hollywood model-actor wannabe?

Then there's the outcry he'll have to deal with from the Religious Right and the televangelists. I can't see Jesus being really thrilled by the way they are representing him. They are certainly going to savage the sweet-faced boy trying to put his hand in their till.

All I can say is, he better have one hell of a website. And he'd better come armed with some bigger, better, and splashier miracles. Just walking on water isn't going to cut it anymore.

What's more, he also is going to have to compete with the levels of insanity provided by reality TV. If he's unlucky enough to land in Vegas first, Penn and Teller will be there to expose how he pulled off the illusion. I don't care if you believe or don't believe, that would really suck for Jesus.

I have to say, though, that this whole concept of the Rapture, of Jesus ushering in his kingdom on earth, sure works well when it looks like the world is on the brink of some form of apocalypse. Not that on any given day it doesn't look that way, but I mean when it really gets cranked up.

Like when Israel and Syria start staring each other down. Or when the cold war was in its heyday and the Russians and the United States stood at the ready, poised with nukes akimbo. Or those moments just before we went after Saddam and his supposed weapons of mass destruction and the "what if" fear that he'd just let them rip.

It was at times like that I definitely took comfort in the Rapture. It sure turns a big negative into one sweet positive.

golfing in the kingdom

I have always had faith in a *something*, in a higher power. It's like the faith I have in the power of appliances to make my life better. It eases my mind.

But there have been experiences in my life that have given me a sense of some sort of higher force, or being, or whatever.

Drugs, for example.

I know, I know, I can hear you. "Don't tell me, Mr. Black, that you are going to advocate the use of drugs." No. Christ on a crutch, no. Why would I do that and spend the rest of my life having to explain myself? All I am saying is that drugs gave me—that's me, no one else—my first introduction to the possibilities of the unseen. Just because I couldn't see it didn't mean it wasn't there. (Read that last line again. I swear, in a very convoluted way it makes sense.)

Look, as much as I hate to say it, because our society so heavy-handedly judges a statement like this, the fact of the matter is that LSD, mushrooms, mescaline, and psilocybin gave me a powerful sense that everything is interconnected.

That's just me again, no one else. (Even though I know now that I am connected to everyone else.) Everything from the infinitesimal interior of the atom to the vastness of the universe, and everything in between—is all of one substance. I could feel it in the very fiber of my being.

"Drugs did this for you?" you may ask. Drugs gave you a "real" sense of a higher power that somehow is at the center of the union of all we survey, leaving you with a sense of awe at its magnificence and splendor? Sorry, but they did. They also gave me a sense that there was a really fine line between sanity and insanity, so a little experimentation went a long way and was more than enough.

I first had an inkling of the possibilities of these mind-expanding drugs in high school, when reports of Timothy Leary, a noted Harvard professor who was working with LSD, started to filter into the media. At the same time, in my chemistry class, my friend Don Smith had the brilliant idea to write, for one of our assignments, on the subject of LSD and similar drugs, like mescaline and mushrooms. Talk about a fun paper to write. My interest had been piqued, so when my pal Charley Rock came back with some mescaline after a college break, I joyously scarfed it down with him. It was cavalier of me, I know, but I had a guide, and I had read Don Smith's paper, so I was ready for anything. And except for the brief flashes of paranoia—thinking that I would be in this condition for the rest of my life—I had a ball. God, it was fun.

Delusional? For sure. An escape from reality? You bet.

And to quote my friend Steve Olsen—who says about any great experience—in the alphabet of fun, it was an A.

Was it a real experience? Who knows? But I know it made me wonder what was real and what truly mattered, what was important and timeless. Like for Alice, the doors just kept opening, and the Cheshire cat Charley Rock kept grinning. The specifics of that day are not nearly as important as the fact that for the first time in my life I felt a sense of transcendence.

There were a few more trips taken on LSD, psilocybin, and mushrooms. They all reinforced the feelings of that first trip, and soon I felt there was nothing to be gained from their continued use. So I stopped.

When I experimented with drugs, I didn't talk to God. I didn't feel like I *was* God. It just became obvious that there was something at work out there and that maybe I shouldn't piss it off. It gave me a sense of peace I hadn't found in any part of the Bible or at any religious service I attended or during any religious education I had.

Until golf.

I never thought that golf could be a spiritual experience, until I had one while playing a round.

Golf for me is normally an afternoon filled with disappointment and self-hatred. It certainly is a game designed for people who don't hate themselves enough in their daily lives, so they play a game that gives them the opportunity to torture themselves. RELENTLESSLY. I play it because it's a vacation from my brain. I spend the day filling it to the brim with inane thoughts such as "Just relax and breathe through your ass." For sheer punishment, golf is a game that never disappoints.

One afternoon about eight years ago, I went with my close friend Bill Foeller to play a round of golf at the first course I ever played as a kid. It's just a place to whack a ball around and where a young kid could pretend he was playing the last nine holes of the Masters and was going to lose the championship, yet again, on the last hole. As a child even my fantasies were unfulfilling. It was across the street from where we lived and on the grounds of what was then the Naval Ordnance Laboratory in White Oak, Maryland, where my father worked. It was a very simple and short nine-hole course and wasn't really much to look at.

For my bar mitzvah, my Uncle Julie had given me his old set of Wilson clubs, so I started playing the course two to three times a week. I had a few lessons at the local recreation center and figured with that as a basis I could teach myself the sport. I knew that many of the greats of golf were self-taught. But they were better teachers than I. I once asked my mother why, since she knew how much I loved to play the game, she never got me lessons. She said that they had gotten me piano lessons and now I hated the piano. She didn't want me to hate golf, too.

I played the course a few times a week because it was one

of the few places, outside of the bathroom, where I could get away by myself. Since I never got any better, no matter how much I played, I guess I enjoyed the frustration.

Yet somehow the nine holes that Bill and I played on that late-summer afternoon were absolutely magical. We played at twilight—trust me, I never notice the light—and we were bathed in an absolutely lovely golden glow. It was sublime. We were the only people playing the course in what I can only call a blissful serenity. Strange, really, and we both took note of it, since one of us was usually bitching about his game. I have even been known to scream on a golf course. (I know that must come as a real shock to you. Me screaming out of frustration. Lewis, surely you jest. On occasion, to underscore a particularly profanity-laced tirade, I have even thrown my clubs, to let people know that my shitty play was their fault, not mine.)

Even stranger, we were accompanied by animals on nearly every hole. This was a course where I rarely remember seeing a squirrel. Now forest creatures were everywhere. It was like something out of a Disney cartoon. Rabbits bounded around us. Mini-deer (or creatures that looked like miniature deer) trailed at a safe distance. Birds of all sorts were hopping on the greens. We even saw an eagle (or maybe it was a hawk; I am no Audubon). Chipmunks and even a few normal-sized deer kept a benevolent eye on us. I can only describe our round as delicious, a word I would never apply to the game. It seemed that what was happening as we made our way from hole to hole was more than a game. Something else was going on. I remember thinking, quite clearly, that it felt as if we were playing in heaven. The kind of heaven one might imagine as a child or if one had the kind of naïve view of heaven that some Christians seem to have, the one pictured in the children's books you'd find at a Christian bookstore. Only Jesus wasn't there as the golf pro. It was heaven if one were a totally obsessed golfer.

I, who have never believed in heaven or hell, believe that Bill and I were in heaven that day on the golf course at the Naval Ordnance Laboratory.

Within a year of that game, my friend Bill died of a heart attack. It was 1999 and he was only fifty-two. He had just had a physical and gotten a clean bill of health. It was one of those events that shock you to your very core. We were supposed to leave the next day for a golf vacation with a few other friends.

Whenever I think of Bill, I see him on the ninth green, getting ready to putt. And it doesn't matter if he sinks it, because we were at total peace in a realm beyond space and time. And Bill knows it, too: I see him on the green, a huge warm smile on his face.

19th newark airport breakdown

As I was writing this book, I found myself at the Newark airport getting ready to fly from New York to Chapel Hill. It was the beginning of June and newspapers were already screaming that it was going to be the worst summer to travel in recorded history. This followed the previous summer, which was then the worst summer on record to travel. If you know something is going to go wrong and you know why something is going to go wrong and you've already experienced the pain and trauma of it going wrong, wouldn't you make a profoundly concerted effort to avoid it happening again? Isn't that just common fucking sense?

Why the hell do we stand with our mouths wide open in wonder, saying, "Wow, it's going to happen again. I knew it was going to happen again, I just didn't believe I was that smart"? Wouldn't you think after you watched the shit hit the fan once, you would move the fan so that when the shit flew again—as it always does—the fan won't get hit?

What the fuck is going on? We have an organization in place that's supposed to deal with this travel problem. It's called the Federal Aviation Administration. Can someone explain to me what it is these people actually do? What do they do in the office all day, make shitballs and throw them at the fan?

They know, for starters, that they need more air traffic controllers. Those poor bastard traffic controllers, who, like teachers, are overworked and underpaid, are of vital importance and are stressed like lab rats testing methedrine. So why wouldn't you hire more air traffic controllers? Is it so difficult a concept to grasp, especially when the last person you want to be exhausted on the job is the one who's guiding big fucking planes around, filled to the teats with passengers and gasoline and zipping around the skies at 400 miles per hour? Terrorists couldn't concoct a better scenario for creating potential mayhem and death. They must be awestruck by the work of the FAA.

If this weren't enough for the terrorists to admire, we are trying to fly too many planes at the same time. The system is overloaded. Is the FAA an extension of the torture staff at Guantánamo?

Wouldn't you like to ensure that, apart from unforeseen problems, a plane would leave and arrive on time and out of harm's way? Do those who work for the FAA ever get on a plane, or do they take the bus? Do they ever have to sit there, strapped to a seat designed by someone with scoliosis, and listen to the captain tell them he'll be back in fifteen minutes to tell them he will be back in fifteen minutes to tell them that a scientific study had proven that fifteen minutes was the longest amount of time you could tell someone they would have to wait for more information about their flight and that this could be repeated indefinitely without the person gouging his ears until the blood poured from them and that he would be back again in fifteen minutes, as soon as he heard from the air traffic controller, who had told him it would be just fifteen more minutes, really, truly?

If it wasn't the pilot telling me that it would be fifteen minutes, it was the airline's representative who was saying the same thing, and it helped to pass a nice chunk of the FOURTEEN HOURS it took to get from Newark to Chapel Hill. How do you turn an hour-and-a-half flight into the equivalent of a journey to Bosnia? BY OVERSCHEDULING AND UNDERPLANNING!

First, the plane I am supposed to be on arrives late from Seattle. So when I finally get on the plane that was supposed to leave at two o'clock and is now supposed to leave at four o'clock, I believe all will be right with the world. Then someone on the ground discovers a mechanical malfunction that can't be fixed. (If you were in midair when you were told this, you'd be praying—hard. But now, on the ground you're thinking, "Go for it, it's just a malfunction, how bad could it be? Dear God, just don't send me back into that airport terminal.")

So at five-fifteen every one of us on the plane gets off. We are told that at this point there is no plan B, which is always a comfort, much like when someone has been killed by lightning and his loved ones are told that God works in mysterious ways. No shit.

At six o'clock, in order to stave off imminent rioting, someone from the airline tells us we are to be given an $8 meal voucher, which would be good for a meal in, let's say, Bangladesh. Here at the Newark airport, where the area's already inflated prices are astronomical, $8 translates into a McDonald's meal that is guaranteed to give you a kind of gaseous nausea that at one time I was actually addicted to. It's the kind of sensation you'd get if you just ate a Styrofoam cup. So why would you eat such a meal? Because after five hours in an airport, one begins to feel just a teensy bit suicidal.

At seven p.m., hope is sparked again when some new chirpy airline employee announces that a new plane without that nasty mechanical problem—the aviation equivalent of the clap—will arrive at nine o'clock. Apparently the old plane would now be used as a decoy plane so that when a plane wasn't available it could be loaded with passengers who could sit there thinking that they would be leaving in fifteen minutes.

Our new departure time is 9:40, but we must now move to a new gate. Yes, why not? The new scenery will be invigorating, and it's right across from a kiosk that sells "I Love NY" paraphernalia. Goody, I'll stock up.

On the way, I pass the airport chapel. What do people pray for in the airport?

The plane arrives at 9:40 and we board by 10:40. By 10:50 I am asleep. I awaken at 11:50. Oh boy, I think, almost there.

I look out the window and there is the ever-present line of planes.

At that point my brain began to eat itself because it had run out of things to do so it turned on itself and my only thought wasn't a thought, it was the color red.

And so at 2:15 a.m., we landed at the Raleigh-Durham Airport, my shirt soaked with my drool. I was a broken man. (If I were a POW and the enemy wanted to torture me for information vital to the security of our armed forces, all they would have to do is show me a picture of an airport. Any airport. Anywhere. And I'd fuck my country over like a pitbull in heat.)

How did the airline explain our late arrival?

There was a "computer glitch" affecting all flights that day.

You have got to be fucking kidding me. A computer glitch? How can major computer systems of any sort not have a backup system in place, making glitches non-fucking-existent? For crying out loud, you can make movies with a home PC that you can upload so that the entire population of India can watch them and no airline system can program a backup? Bullllllshiiiit.

It's like inventing fire and not keeping something lit in case the main fire goes out. If our ancestors were as dumb as we are, we wouldn't be here. No wonder we can't deal with the truly difficult problems like poverty, universal health care, or world peace.

Why do I bring this up (besides in order to get the taste of bile I am choking on out of my mouth)? Well, it's because I believe that if the Christians are correct and there truly is a hell, then Satan presides over his flock at an exact replica of any airport in America. You spend an eternity wandering from gate to gate to gate, until you finally get onto planes that never take off, carrying vouchers for food you cannot swallow without gagging, wearing a busted iPod, awash in a series of announcements that have absolutely no meaning because any idiot would know not to do any of the things you're being told not to do. "Be absolutely sure to pull your penis out before urination and aim at the white porcelain receptacle, not at the tile."

You don't burn in this hell; you sweat constantly, but ever so slightly, and you smell like a piece of rancid meat, and as a result your genitals itch just enough to be painful when you scratch them, which is continually. You are too tired to be awake and too awake to sleep. Your memory offers no comfort, for it is filled only with shadows and the voice of your mother saying, "Didn't I *tell* you?"

an airline traveler's prayer

O Heavenly Father, who in Your wisdom created airplanes so that man could be like unto a retarded bird with a broken wing, please move things along and truly give unto us the miracle of teleportation. I don't know how much longer I can take this. Once I enter the doors of the airport, Heavenly Father, I fear that there will come a time when I will no longer be responsible for my own actions. I can no longer abide my spirit being extinguished in the name of airport security. I don't want to take off my shoes. My shoes hold nothing but my feet. I can no longer watch as they molest the elderly in the name of safety. In the name of Christ, Your only begotten son, my hair gel doesn't come in a container that is 3.4 ounces or less. I don't care that we are now in Code Orange, I have no orange to wear. I am losing my fucking mind in here. I want to tear off my clothes and run on all fours onto the tarmac and bark at the planes like a dog.

Do You hear me, Heavenly Father? Can You feel my plight? I know it's not much in the scheme of things, but I am here four or five times a week, and I fear one of these days I will no longer be responsible for my own actions. It could happen on the plane, when they show, on those tiny screens—which make me wonder why You ever gave us the gift of sight—a movie that could only have been made to play for cows in order to increase their production of milk. My own nipples fill to bursting as I watch it, filling with a black venom that I fear will spurt out onto my neighbor's bag of snack nuggets.

Am I making myself clear to You, who maintains order in the universe, except in airport baggage claim, so I can always be certain that the wait for my luggage is actually longer than my flight time?

And so as I stand here waiting, wondering if I will ever see my hair gel again, I try to have pure thoughts. Thoughts that will lift me above the base animal urges I feel, like running up the conveyor belt to rip out the heart of an innocent baggage handler to assuage the burning in my skull. But higher thoughts don't come, O Lord. So I turn my anger on myself, and I find myself wanting to rip my eyes from their sockets so I will no longer have to bear witness to the insanity I am watching.

The conveyor belt is empty, O Lord, it is empty. It isn't even moving. Please move my conveyor belt, the one that rises up into the heavens and brings me closer to You. Amen.

ron the archangel

I will repeat, briefly, a story I've related elsewhere, as it was another spiritual encounter that has shaped the way I look at religion.

I was at my younger brother Ron's bedside just after he passed away. I stared at his ashen, lifeless body and knew that he was gone. Yet his spirit filled the room. I felt it all around me. It was so strong that I knew he was still there.

In this moment of extreme loss, I was comforted by him, by his presence.

I never expected that.

I am not someone who believes in ghosts or angels. And yet at that moment I felt something completely inexplicable and unlike anything I knew or believed up to that point in my life.

Within a few months of Ron's death in July 1997, career doors that had been closed to me began to swing open. I have no doubt that my brother was the one who was helping to unlock them. How? I haven't a clue. What I do know is that my work as a comic began to be noticed. When I went to clubs on the road, there were now lines outside to see me. There were calls to my manager from television producers who had taken no interest in me before. I was asked to perform at the HBO Comedy Festival in Aspen. Within months a call came out of the blue asking if I could put on a one-man show—it was produced off-Broadway and called *Black Humour.*

No doubt some would say that I was finally reaping the rewards for my work, or that things were naturally falling into place, or that it was just the luck of the draw. I say it was my brother, working in mysterious ways.

It's just like religion: You believe what you want to believe.

$e=mc^2$

When I sensed that my brother was still in the room after he died, it reinforced a belief I had. Or let's call it a feeling. A belief just sounds too heavy.

When Ron passed, I felt with all of my being that while the body dies, we don't really go anywhere because we're just this collection of energy. The religious would prefer to call it the soul, or the spirit, but I call it energy.

And the great thing about energy is that it doesn't go away, because it has nowhere to go. (Maybe it doesn't have a driver's license.) It doesn't die. It just becomes something else.

Now, for all I know it becomes a butcher-block table, but also maybe it remains conscious, and wouldn't it be hell to be a conscious butcher-block table?

From what I gather, these are basic laws of physics, but I didn't take physics in college because it was a tough subject, and as far as the sciences went I had the brainpower of a butcher-block table. It would have been nice if I had studied it, so I could clear all this up for the reader and myself.

At times when I am truly nuts, I think that we are always here. That every moment you've existed remains in space. Every nanosecond of time remains. Everything that has ever happened continues to happen, from the beginning of time to the end of time, simultaneously. It is a never-ending chain of events. It's why people think they can go back in time and into the future. A lot of science-fiction tales are based on this idea. It's an idea that I think might be real. I can't explain it, I just feel it.

But like I said, I am crazy.

virtual reality

In the summer of 2007, I read an article by John Tierney in *The New York Times*. In it he quoted Dr. Nick Bostrom, the head of the Future of Humanity Institute at Oxford University. This is what the good doctor had to say:

"My gut feeling, and it's nothing more than that, is that there's a 20 percent chance we're living in a computer simulation."

A thought like that is enough to bring an end to my day.

All of this world is just a computer simulation? I get shooting pains behind my eyes just thinking about the possibility. If you thought that, Mr. Big-Shot Doctor, why would you tell anyone?

So I am not the creation of a just and loving God, but of some angst-ridden thirteen-year-old kid who instead of taking the edge off his life by masturbating has come up with a virtual world that he loves to torment.

But what if it's fucking true? Think of the implications.

I have never had sex with anybody; I never appeared on *The Daily Show* or made any movies, and I never won a Grammy Award. My life would really suck. Or, as the case may be, it would virtually suck. On the upside, however, my ex-wife would never have existed. In the big picture, not a bad trade-off.

Still, why am I running around the country performing? Why am I killing myself writing this book? This makes existentialism look like the Playboy Philosophy. To be perfectly honest, I'd rather believe in intelligent design than that we're all living in some kind of video game.

It doesn't end there. John Tierney poses the nightmarish question: What if the designer of this simulation is a virtual being, too? And what if he is living in a simulation operated by another virtual being? And what if it's ad infinitum?

Jesus! It was thoughts like these that made me stop doing drugs.

the truth shall make you free

As the heady, turbulent, confusing sixties wound down and lurched into the much more complacent seventies, with its incessantly annoying disco beat, many of my generation turned their attention away from hedonistic indulgences and toward more spiritual pursuits. Somewhere among the drugs and the music and the growing paranoia of the times—or perhaps it was just the overwhelming sense of hopelessness, since we naïvely believed we would change the world and our legacy seemed to be long hair and bell-bottoms—the next logical step seemed to be in the direction of religion. If you could NOT change the outer world, the theory went, maybe you could change your inner one.

When you think you're going to change the world and ultimately you find out that it's just not going to be possible when your president and Congress don't really give a shit, and you aren't going to participate in an armed revolution or start another food co-op, the search for an underlying and immutable force starts to make sense.

Maybe that's why a marked resurgence of Christianity took place a few decades later. If you can't change this world for the better, then you'd better find peace for yourself in the next one. In much the same way that my generation had a voice in the issues of the day disproportionate to our size, so the Christian Right has been enjoying an outsized influence during Bush the Younger's ruthless reign. Or at least thought they were, as much has been written about how the administration used them. (In the end, we both took it in the ass. I doubt the Christian Right would like to hear it put that way.)

Back in the 1960s I had an experience that I would call spiritual. I had been given a playwriting fellowship, so after I graduated from college, I stayed on in Chapel Hill for a year and began working on a play with a few of my fellow students. During that time, I began to read a book by Alan Watts called *The Taboo Against Knowing Yourself.* In many ways it was a very simple, even simplistic, view of how to live a more spiritual life. But simplistic or not, I took from it a major life lesson: Always tell the truth.

As I said, it wasn't what you would call complicated reading. But I took the book's advice.

For the first time in my life, I stumbled onto the concept of faith.

Maybe I was just trying it on for size, as a way to allay my fears over writing the play. I remember being decidedly nervous about whether the play would be any good. Whatever the reason, it worked. I believed that all would be revealed, and it was.

What exactly it was that was revealed, I have no earthly clue anymore. And, quite frankly, who cares? But I do remember feeling okay about things at the time. I have never experienced anything like it before or since.

Even now, as I stare at this half-empty page, I try to bring that naïve faith back into my life. "All will be revealed," my faith tells me. "The page will be filled." But at my age, and with the knowledge of the experience, my brain just laughs at me, as if to say, "Good fucking luck."

But back in the seventies, things were very different. It was an extraordinary time. I never doubted that I would eventually fill those empty pages with the play that I needed to write. My brain had focused on telling a story, and my subconscious, supported by my faith, relaxed enough to listen. No matter where I turned at the time, I found an answer. If it wasn't the answer itself, it was something that led me to the answer. The faith gave me a certainty that I have never known with my writing. I understand now when people talk about how God revealed a path to them: It is faith that initiates the revelation of the path.

And, in turn, faith can produce all sorts of miracles. It just seems to take a major miracle to find the faith and hold on to it. Especially in a world where there is so much information swirling around that you've got a perpetual howling in your ear.

"What's that, faith? Is that you, faith? I can hardly hear

you." Hey, it's hard to keep the faith when it only speaks in a whisper.

It wasn't just the play that was affected—and it turned out to be a hit, by the way—but my life was changed. If someone needed advice, I knew exactly what to tell them, and I had no fear of doing so, because I knew I was speaking the truth.

How did I know? Because I spoke whatever was on my mind without taking into account the feelings of the other person.

I actually thought people would appreciate my brand of honesty. I'm not so sure that they did. One thing is for certain, however: Whatever I was doing made me feel high. It wasn't a stoned high, just a very clearheaded one.

And then one day it all went up in smoke.

I will never forget it. We were performing the play in Charlotte, North Carolina, and I was asked by a young professor from UNC-Charlotte to join him and his wife for drinks at their home after the show. I accepted and showed up with Gayle, an actress in the play I was hopelessly in love with. (I was the playwright, she was the actress—oh, the unrequited clichéd love of it all.) The prof wanted to pick my brain. He was a professor of Black Studies at the university, and he and his wife were white. Apparently the university administration had been unable to find any African-Americans in North Carolina. It happens.

Anyway, here he was, an upper-middle-class white man

teaching middle-class white students about a black underclass he could never truly understand since, well, he was white. Let's just say he had something of an internal conflict going on.

I knew exactly what advice to give him. I was twenty-two years old and a recent college graduate. I knew it all. I told him that he had to find a way to reconcile his lifestyle with his beliefs. Was I brilliant or what?

Of course, when pressed, I had to admit that I didn't know what he could do to bring about this reconciliation. And that's when it struck me: I'm only twenty-two and barely out of college—I know absolutely nothing! Who was I to pass judgment or hand out advice? Where were the adults giving me advice?

But I couldn't tell this professor the truth. All I could tell him was what he wanted to hear, which was that he was on the right track. So I told him that. I told him what would make him feel good.

It was at that precise moment in time that my faith evaporated, and from then on I found it harder and harder to tell the truth. I have spent my life trying to get back to the way I lived then.

As insane as I know this sounds, I felt that I had been completely in tune with the universe. Now I feel totally out of step. Slightly disconnected from everything and everyone. Ain't life grand?

age of disenlightenment

It was the Beatles who played a large part in bringing to our shores religious figures from the East. The incredibly influential rockers had taken a trip to India in 1968 and had hooked up with the Maharishi Mahesh Yogi and his path to enlightenment, called Transcendental Meditation. The group's trip was one long commercial for the Godhead.

By the time the Maharishi hit Stateside, people were lining up to see him. Imagine if the Beatles had embraced Islam, the way Cat Stevens did. Who knows where we would be now. We might have avoided September 11, or maybe we just would have attacked ourselves.

So once the word of the successful tour of the Maharishi got back to India, the floodgates burst open. First there were the Hare Krishnas, who inundated this country's streets and airports with tambourines, sandals, and outstretched hands. And let's face it, they had to love God if they were going to look like that. Saffron robes and bald heads with ponytails. They make the geek of today look GQ.

Not to be outdone, we even started to grow our own gurus here.

It was all about enlightenment. This worked well for the mind-set that wanted the perks of religion without having to deal with God. Or if there was going to have to be a God, then at least you could see his embodiment here on earth.

One of the first of these new snake charmers I had contact with was the Guru Maharaji. It was Gayle who led me to him. Sitting at his feet was the last place I wanted to be, but unrequited love plays strange tricks on the brain, and, as any man knows, it sure can do a number on the penis.

Gayle had written to me that she was in London and was now a follower of a thirteen-year-old guru. She had become a member of his dance company. Thirteen years old and the kid's a guru? You've got to be kidding me. At least that was my first thought. And then my second. And my third. My fourth thought was that the guy has got to be a midget. For God's sake, that's the age I was bar mitzvahed. How does someone with acne lead anyone along a spiritual path? (Oh, if I had only known this when I was bar mitzvahed. I could have become the world's only thirteen-year-old rabbi, moved to Los Angeles, started a congregation, and really gotten my career off to a speedy start.)

It was tough enough for me to stand in front of family and friends, reading from the Torah and the Haftorah in Hebrew, and then translating the passage and explaining what it all meant to me. And this kid was in charge of his own religious group? Or a cult. But a cult of what? Clearasil? Doesn't a religious leader need a driver's license? Christ, by thirteen I hadn't even figured out how to masturbate. I didn't know how to please myself, let alone worry about pleasing God.

I was in a bit of a panic about Gayle, so I called her in England. She seemed completely content, even serene. I threw out a few arguments about the idiocy of following a thirteen-year-old guru, but to no avail.

"Are you sure you haven't lost your mind?" I asked.

"No," she said joyously, "I have found it."

Oh, sweet Jesus, I said to myself.

Gayle is one of the most sublime and wondrous creatures I have ever met on this planet. I would seek out her new bar mitzvah boy and see what he was up to, in the hope that I'd understand what my dear friend had gotten herself into.

The first contact I made with the boy wonder was in Colorado, at a huge festival in his honor. Apparently many of the folks saw the guru as the Lord of the Universe. With a thirteen-year-old Lord, I thought, this must be a pretty young universe. I wasn't buying it. A thirteen-year-old Lord, awash in the changes brought on by puberty, fuck!

What I remember most vividly is he seemed to be hanging around with some hot stewardesses and he had a Rolls-Royce and a couple of other swell cars that he wasn't old enough to drive. These cars—and their drivers—didn't seem so spiritual to me, but I was told he had no attachment to them, so it wasn't a sign of his materialism.

How do you argue with logic like that? I just figured this new Lord of the Universe was no idiot. What's he going to be driven around in, a Pontiac? Or to quote the Bible: "And the Lord saw the Rolls-Royce, and it was a bitchin' ride."

This was back in the early seventies, before conspicuous consumption became a good thing. A Rolls was an unusual sight, especially at a religious festival. And what was the kid dispensing that was enabling him to raise the money for a Rolls—and apparently a lot more? It was called, I shit you not, The Knowledge.

The Knowledge. The Secret. The Truth. They've always got a name for whatever they're selling as "The Way." Most of my adulthood, I have preferred The Secret Truth for Making the Perfect Martini. There's my path to enlightenment.

The Knowledge, as it turned out, was four different ways to meditate, and by doing so you could achieve inner peace. All you had to do to receive The Knowledge was attend a few meetings and then sign up for the all-day session, where it would be given out to you. There was no charge for this. Actually you were asked to bring a piece of fruit, like an apple. I guess once they had you hooked, they would go after the cash, like a heroin dealer who gives you the first free dose up front. Or maybe The Knowledge compelled you to give your money to the kid.

I had to see for myself just what this Knowledge was. So

when I moved to Maryland to work in a theater company, I went to a number of meetings of his followers at an ashram in Washington, D.C. These meetings were called Satsangs, and it was at them that the converts talked about their experiences with The Knowledge or how they felt about the kid. They were all grinning that grin that one finds only in the zealously religious. The kind of grin that says idiocy has replaced any form of real thought.

These people were all harmless enough, and like any group that seeks converts, they were thrilled to have me around. They treated me like just one more moron to throw on the pyre of enlightenment.

The meetings were run by one of the kid's disciples, who were all from India. Even in his pidgin English, the disciple seemed a lot more spiritual than his fearless leader. For starters, he was a lot older than thirteen, and that was comforting. He wasn't surrounded by a circus of sycophants and a luxury car dealership. He also gave off the impression that he was completely at peace and at one with the universe. Finally, as he spoke of the meditation, he exuded truth and wisdom.

On the day I was to receive The Knowledge, I brought my apple and placed it in the basket. I was so skeptical about this, I'll bet you could have smelled it on me. Our teacher that day was actually my favorite of the guru's disciples, and he blew my cynical mind when he meditated in front of us and within thirty seconds of his beginning to meditate his skin became translucent, as if a light were shining through it. If that was a magic trick, it was fucking spectacular. No one commented on it; the room was absolutely silent.

Once he had finished meditating, it was time for us to be given our four meditative techniques. I will not go through them for you. You want The Knowledge, cough up your own goddamn apple.

I will tell you that we were told to close our eyes. Without going into details, I was instructed to focus on where my third eye would be. Easy enough. I had two eyes in my head, and there was the one-eyed monster in my pants. That made three. I was focused.

You weren't supposed to watch as the instructor went from pupil to pupil, but I snuck a few peeks. He was barely touching anyone. So when he came to me, I am sure he was doing the same thing, but the effect was overwhelming: When he touched me, it was as if he had poked my eyes as hard as he could. It was such an overwhelming jolt that I felt as if my head was going to explode. The vague shapes and shadowy figures I had been seeing turned into a mandala of spectacularly vivid colors. My mind was seriously blown. If I was going to meditate, this was the meditation for me.

I know I don't seem like the kind of person who would meditate, but at least I now had begun to understand what had attracted Gayle to this outfit. It seemed pretty powerful, and I wanted to see where it would lead me. Despite my earlier skepticism, I actually found it fascinating. It seemed to be a gateway to the power of the mind.

Still, it didn't seem all that spiritual to me, and it was totally separate from the thirteen-year-old kid. He was just the pitchman. Besides, it only cost an apple. I had paid a lot more for a lot less.

So every afternoon, I sat upright and put a sheet over my head. (Don't even ask.) The first four times I meditated, not much happened. My body was no doubt adjusting to staying still for a half hour. Then, as now, I am not good at sitting still. I've always been a twitcher. But the fifth time I got under the sheet, all hell broke loose. Bright colors were spinning in circles and everything around me was blue—sky blue to be exact.

"Holy shit," my conscious flashed, "I'm in the sky. I AM IN THE FUCKING SKY. It smells like the outdoors. And there's a cloud."

It freaked the piss out of me. And just as soon as I realized I was in the sky, I wasn't anymore.

That was that. I never tried to meditate again. That's how much it shook me up. It's one thing to watch someone's tie turn into a snake while you're on some hallucinogen; it's quite another thing to be sober and float around in the sky while your body is in the living room.

It is the only out-of-body experience I have ever had. I know I was in the sky. I know I saw that cloud. No one ever talked about this kind of experience at Satsang. And that was the problem. These guys knew how to hook us up to our interior, but they didn't seem to know how to guide us out. They didn't really communicate how the interior reality and the exterior reality could be brought into balance. They didn't warn us that we would be tripping our brains out. At least the first guy who gave me mescaline gave me that little talk beforehand. I call that responsible.

Now, my grip on reality has always been tenuous at best. I'm the kind of person who needs balance. I have always taken my cues from what I see around me. It's my guide. And if I was going to be going God knows where when I closed my eyes, I needed a reliable guide. Not some thirteen-year-old sitting in the back of a Rolls-Royce.

I never talked to Gayle about this. I didn't have to: The unrequited love died in the sky. I went from serious meditation back to heavy masturbation.

I found they both do the job. They calm you down.

the american guru

At about the same time the kid from India was making his way around the United States, there was an American guru-in-waiting hitting the highways in a big yellow school bus. I had heard about him from my brother, who had seen him in Ann Arbor, and the word about him was spreading quickly. It's amazing how, even without the Internet, one used to pick up information. I guess people used to talk more. Even to each other.

Stephen Gaskin was a spiritual leader who came out of San Francisco. He had an exceptional understanding of hallucinogens and their effects, and he was very clear when he explained them. It was nice to have some clarity on drugs that were still a mystery in many ways. So, armed with that information and the vision it had given him, he gathered his followers into a bus caravan, no doubt inspired by Ken Kesey, who had made the idea of the bus famous. ("You're either on the bus or off the bus.") Gaskin and his followers crossed the country to preach their vision of a better life. Wherever he went, he gathered new followers, who bought their own buses and joined him on his journey.

I had never thought of a big yellow school bus as something I would ever want to get into again. Does anyone have good school bus memories? (Now he was leading a spiritual convoy across country, like some insane class trip.)

As anyone with a message does, Stephen and his bus caravan came through Washington, D.C.—attracted, no doubt, by the fact that the government resides there. (Who knows? You might convert a congressman or two.) Living just outside D.C. at the time, I couldn't pass up the opportunity to see if Gaskin was a wise man or just another snake oil salesman. (You never know when you might need some snake oil. Even if just to keep the toilet bowl sparkling white.)

So Ron, my brother, my friends Lenny and Cliff, Cliff's girlfriend, Dee-Dee, and I headed out to hear what Stephen had to say. The gathering was held at the All Souls Unitarian Church in downtown Washington, D.C. (The Unitarians have always been good this way. They are open to all things spiritual. It's the believe-whatever-you-want denomination.) There we joined folks of all shapes and sizes and descriptions, from worried parents to hippies to wannabes. There were not a lot of suits in attendance.

As I remember it, Stephen gave a lucid and insightful talk about the world we were living in and how we could change it through what we learned from our drug experiences. Then he opened the floor for questions, many of which were about personal psychedelics. And like a new age Dr. Phil (but without the smarminess), he answered them. Our government, when it came to marijuana and hallucinogens, spent its time freaking people out rather than helping everyone to understand what they might be taking and how they might be able to deal with the power of such drugs. (Maybe this could have been done during arrests for drug possession. Instead of being read their rights, suspects could be given some tips on how to deal with alternate realities.) But dispensing valuable information has never been our government's strong suit.

Stephen then went on to describe a utopian vision of a farm that his group had purchased in Tennessee. He invited everyone listening to join up and settle there. They would live off the land and become a self-contained community.

Okay. I know. Nowadays, when there is usually an MBA within ten feet of you, this sounds not only insane but impossible. Who the fuck would give up everything to follow a drug-taking, long-haired, and bearded hippy?

What can I say? It was another century, another time. And maybe, just maybe, people were a little more open to alternative lifestyles.

And which is crazier: an ever-growing population of greedy pricks who can't see the social good through the jungle of designer crap that's everywhere as they transform the idea of "keeping up with the Joneses" into "keeping up with the Sun King"? Or a bunch of young people, mostly suburban born and bred, who have never even thought of farming but who jump onto school buses and head toward Tennessee because they are dissatisfied with their lives? Okay, let's call it a toss-up.

(I am sure that many of you reading this find it unbelievable that such a caravan could exist and that on a whim people would pick up their lives and move on. This has happened throughout the history of the world, as well as the history of America. Idealists or religious leaders or nut jobs all have presented another vision of life, and those who are dissatisfied with the one they're living have packed up and headed toward a new one. Religion is based on dissatisfaction with the real world. We don't see so much of it now, I guess, because everyone is so fucking happy.)

The whole idea captured my friend Cliff's imagination, though maybe not as much as it did his girlfriend's. It was an extraordinary alternative—and about as alternative as you could get, considering that Cliff was living in a suburban Maryland apartment complex and was looking for some direction in his life. So in just a matter of days, he and Dee-Dee joined the caravan.

As for me, I couldn't have done it, as I thought I was going to be a playwright. Besides, I would rather kill myself than be a farmer. That's not to disparage farming; I am just not built for it, as I need to be indoors as much as possible. And having to start a community from scratch, which on paper might sound thrilling, has no appeal to me. None. Zero. My pioneer spirit leans toward the mental, not the physical, and it extends exactly as far as the Internet will take me. If I had to get on one of those wooden boats to get here the way the first European settlers did, I would have taken one look at it and said, "Fuck it, who needs freedom?"

Hedging his bets, Cliff said to us, "See you in a couple of weeks," and he and Dee drove off in their big yellow school bus, as if they were on their way to a Partridge Family reunion. I think it was the path to enlightenment that was attractive to Cliff, and sometimes the path leads to Tennessee. The fact was, the people in the caravan were looking to lead a more spiritual life, one not necessarily defined by God or the rules of organized religion. And do you need God to lead a spiritual life? I suppose so, if you're desperate for an authority figure who's invisible but can be tasted at communion. Can't you just practice what Jesus preaches and live a good and upright life? Isn't that spiritual enough? What if you did do that and because you didn't believe in God, he sent you to hell? Well, for me that would sure justify not believing in him in the first place, especially if he's going to be such a prick.

Cliff and I kept sporadically in touch while he and Dee were on the road. He returned home at one point for a visit, and our old clique (we called ourselves a clique in semimockery of the elitism of it all) got together with him. It was a strained meeting, as we each had different opinions of Cliff's new life, mainly because it wasn't our life and we didn't know anything about it. For starters, on the farm you were referred to by your proper name. Cliff was Clifford and Dee-Dee was now once again Anita. That was tough to take. He was a Cliff, not a Clifford. No one's a Clifford, are they? Maybe if you're British.

When someone you have known and been close to for years, who was nurtured in the system, so to speak, leaves the system, judgments are passed on both sides.

"How could anyone as smart as you throw your life away like this? Don't you want more?"

"How could anyone as smart as you stay here in the suburbs? What are you thinking? Don't you want more?"

"You're throwing away your education!"

"And what exactly have you done with yours?"

"I thought we were going to change the world."

"I am at least trying to, in my small way."

None of this was spoken. It just hung in the air.

I think what bugged us most was Cliff's submergence of ego in the Farm, which is what they called their community. And then of course there was the idea of a guru, which is what Stephen Gaskin seemed to have become. It was completely foreign to the rest of us. It was similar to having your best friend give up his American citizenship and move to Russia in the fifties. It just wasn't done.

Whether we liked it or not, Cliff was happy.

It could have been worse. He could have been a Moonie.

A year later, another good friend, Jeff Davis, was heading to see his girlfriend in Bloomington, Indiana, to finalize their wedding plans. He asked me to join him on his road trip, and we decided to stop in and see the Farm and Cliff. Jeff saw it as a way to clear his mind, a kind of spiritual tune-up if you will, before the big day. I saw it as an opportunity to see what my pal "Clifford" was up to.

A group of folks greeted us at the Farm's rustic gatehouse, but Cliff and Dee were not among them. The greeters were very gracious, but when they spoke it was always about the group. What mattered to them was Stephen and the Farm and all its inhabitants. What mattered to me was seeing Cliff and Dee-Dee. It was like going to a suburban neighborhood to see a friend and being met by the homeowners association.

The Farm itself was idyllic in a very hippie-esque fashion, a countercultural version of a trailer park. Dirt roads and paths and, yes, school buses were everywhere. The buses were decorated with bright colors and tapestries and had been transformed into homes that poked out of the trees. It was as if *In Watermelon Sugar*, a book by Richard Brautigan, had come to life. There was an undeniable pot smoker's charm to the place, and that is not meant disparagingly. One felt extremely comfortable there. But I wouldn't have wanted to be around if there had been a hurricane, a tornado, or a shortage of pot. (I don't know how this would have all seemed to me if I hadn't had a little bit of a buzz on. I imagine this place could have turned really weird really fast.)

I was thrilled when I finally got to see Cliff and Dee. They were very happy with their new lives. I was working in a theater at that time, which was as close to bohemian as you could get. The theater company Jeff and I were a part of was a communal effort. But Cliff's and Dee's lives made ours look mainstream by comparison. Here were a bunch of well-educated freaks farming while leading a spiritual life with pot. They were certainly moving to the beat of a different drummer.

One of the weirdest concepts being tried out there was a four-marriage. This is where two couples got married. It was polygamy without any of the male-centric advantages one finds in Mormon fundamentalism. Right there in Summertown, Tennessee, the state that gave us the Scopes trial, which debated whether evolution should be taught in public schools, and these folks were looking to evolve. All of this was years before *Desperate Housewives, The L Word,* or *The Sopranos* began to change the openness of the American psyche. I can't imagine the damage the Ku Klux Klan would have done at the Farm if they had known what was going on there.

The four-marriage concept was a real shocker; I hadn't come to grips with the two-marriage yet. Jesus, what do you tell your parents: "I've fallen for a few people"? What would Jesus say? I don't think it would make him very happy. There are just too many permutations to deal with. Who can do the math in that kind of marriage? And (as I go for the dumb joke here) the PMS must be overwhelming. It seemed like a hell of a side road for those on a spiritual journey. Stephen had entered into a four-marriage, and what's good for the guru is good for the gander.

The Farm was also trying another interesting social experiment. For those who were screwups in the community, who weren't following the rules, who got out of line, or who were just a communal pain in the ass, there was the Rock Tumbler. People who broke the rules had to spend time with a group of people who were specially selected to get the transgressor back on the communal track. Basically it was a group of people who were fun, people who weren't, and people who would probably bore you to tears. Sounds like a party to me. I don't know, I'd rather tussle with a warthog.

I cannot even discuss the diet on the Farm. The memory of it still causes mild cramping. It was vigilantly vegetarian and was more than my body could bear. I swore I was eating leaves at one point. But when one shares one's bounty with another, one can't complain.

Night fell, and it was magical. Jeff and I walked to where we were staying, a small wooden cabin amidst the buses, whose lights appeared like fireflies through the trees. It was really like another world—a nice world to visit, but I wouldn't want to live there.

The next day, we wandered around the Farm, watching

various farm activities. In the late sixties and seventies—even now, for that matter—there are those who give up their office lives to return to the land, to a quieter and simpler life. (Quieter? Yes. Simpler? In some ways, sure. But there's a ton of shit that goes into making things so simple.) It's a tough life, and these people had started from scratch and were learning along the way. I could see that for my friend Cliff, whose sharp and incisive mind would find working in an office drudgery at best, the Farm was an alternative to dying on the vine. He was now planting vines, but he certainly seemed content. Much more so than if he had been leading the life of a Washington bureaucrat.

That afternoon, the whole group had been summoned for an important meeting with Stephen. It took place on a hillside surrounded by trees, the blue sky and rolling hills as a backdrop. Stephen spoke to the group about a few items on the Farm's agenda. Things that needed to be done, a report from the Rock Tumbler on who was getting out of there and who had to go in. And then Stephen began to talk about his own four-marriage. Apparently the other husband had been having difficulties (who wouldn't?) and was acting out, and this had disturbed Stephen so much that he felt he had no other choice but to banish him from the community, so that the guy could get his head together. (Back in those days we had heads and we had to get them together. Don't ask. It means just what it sounds like it means.) The other husband begged for forgiveness. Stephen was adamant, and it struck me that the four-marriage would now be just a three marriage.

And then it took a real turn to the weird. The other husband said that Stephen either was Jesus Christ or was the incarnation of Jesus.

It was a remark that freaked the shit out of me. It was clear that the guy had been in the woods too long.

I don't remember Stephen denying his divinity, and that didn't sit well on my already overtaxed stomach. But what made the scene even weirder was that while this discussion was going on, I saw a pure white aura around Stephen's head. That put my brain into the spin cycle.

I looked around to see if it was being faked, but there was no way it could have been: We were sitting in the middle of a fucking field. In light of all the information I was receiving, my brain had only one reply: DOES NOT COMPUTE.

We watched as the other husband hit the road. And after what I had seen, I was ready to take the walk with him. The meeting was adjourned, and it was time for supper. Maybe their diet made all of this seem rational to them, but my anus was weeping at the thought of more of that cuisine.

We ate, and Jeff and I headed off to our cabin. I understood why Cliff had come here. I just didn't understand why he was staying. I probably should have tried to talk him out of it, but I doubt I could have. Even a utopia gone bad, like a good marriage gone bad, can be seductive.

As we lay in the dark in our cute little camp beds, I broached the subject that had been bothering me since the meeting.

"Jeff, I know this is going to sound crazy..." I began.

"You saw the white light," he said quietly.

"Oh shit, you did, too?"

"It was coming right out of his head."

"What the fuck was that about?"

"I want a burger."

In retrospect, I think that what we saw was less about divinity than it was about hundreds of people pumping the purest energy of attention toward Stephen, and hence a white light pops out of his head. It came from the folks he was talking to, not from him. He is not the new Messiah. You gotta trust me on this one. (He is not Jesus Christ. Like I said, I don't even believe Jesus Christ was Jesus Christ.)

The next morning, Jeff and I skipped breakfast. As sad as I was to say good-bye to Cliff, since I didn't know when I would see him again, I was overjoyed to be returning to the material world. Without my even suggesting it, as soon as we left the Farm, Jeff stopped at the first restaurant we saw.

It was one of the best burgers I have ever eaten. It wasn't a spiritual experience. It just felt like home.

reincarnation

I must admit that I find the whole idea of reincarnation very attractive. Very attractive, indeed. It works better for me than heaven or hell.

Who could blame me? Let's face it, no one wants to go to hell. Sure, it seems like a place that a lot of people should go, but I don't want to be one of them. There's no argument that it's the right place for Hitler and a lot of his Nazi pals and others of his ilk. But then you have a bunch of duplicitous douche bags thrown in with them. That just doesn't seem logical to me. There's a big difference between being a run-of-the-mill asshole and being a truly evil prick.

Heaven, on the other hand, seems like a nice enough place. I'm just afraid that it seems a little too nice, that I'd just get depressed there with nothing to bitch about. And what kind of an afterlife would that be? I sure would like to be an angel for a while, however, and I even believe that angels have watched over me. Still, I think heaven is merely a way station where you do a little time before you are returned to earth.

That's where reincarnation comes in. Some people don't like the idea because you come back as someone else, but I am comfortable with that. Once as me is enough.

Now, the theory is that who you come back as depends on how evolved you were when you checked out. If you were a prick the first time around, you might come back as a dung beetle or a gnat. If you were a decent human being who tried to do the right thing, you move up the food chain. Seems pretty straightforward to me.

I know it's kind of a crapshoot, but I still like the odds. And I *really* like the fact that you come back here. I like this place. I know it's not perfect, but if I had my choice, I wouldn't want to go to heaven *or* hell. I want to come back here. There are more stories here. And more pricks to deal with. Especially the executive at Fox Television who, after I came in to do a reading with a makeshift cast for a pilot that had been developed for me, said, "If I knew that the lead was going to be Lewis Black, we wouldn't have had this reading. There's no way he can carry a series." I'd like to come back and waste his time and energy, and then kick his ass.

What? Am I missing the point or something?

the psychic

I am rarely shocked by anything, which is why I think this is an important story.

And not to worry, I will not be shocked if any of you don't believe what I am about to tell you. Quite frankly, I won't blame you. Still, I maintain that this is absolutely true, and it's why I believe in something, even though I can't define it.

In 1998, I got a call from Tamara Nerby, a terrific comedienne and a wonderful friend who lives in Minneapolis. She had recently seen a friend of hers named Michael who happened to be a psychic. He didn't know who I was. I wasn't on anyone's radar yet, unless you were a complete comedy junkie, and Michael wasn't one of those.

In the midst of a conversation the two of them were having, Michael said to her, "You know, you have to stop worrying about your friend Lewis. He's going to do just fine. He's going to have a spectacular career, so you don't have to worry about him anymore."

That's when Tamara called me. She assured me that she had never mentioned me to Michael, and therefore I should take this seriously.

I don't know which was the bigger shock. That Michael, who didn't know me from Adam, was now talking about me to a good friend, or that big things were going to happen in my career. In retrospect, I have to say, the second part was much more shocking—and, ultimately, more intriguing.

When this incident happened, my stand-up career was satisfying if not huge, and I had accepted the fact that I was about as successful as I was ever going to be, with maybe a few unexpected goodies along the way. I was a moderately established club comic who had what could generously be called a cult following that had taken years to develop. And I felt that I was lucky enough to be on *The Daily Show* for a year or so. People were just beginning to pay attention to the show, but it was nowhere near the national phenomenon it was to become.

Now, up until this time, I had very little contact with psychics. Friends, and friends of friends, had told stories of extraordinary readings, but nothing like this. Remember, the guy didn't know me.

When I next returned to the Acme Comedy Club in Minneapolis for a week of shows, I asked Tamara to set up a meeting with Michael. Just to thank him for the good news and to see how he knew more than my agents or I did. I felt I needed to know which powers that be out in the universe he was chatting up.

Tamara, Michael, and I met for lunch. I expected it to be very weird, but it wasn't in the least. It was an afternoon filled with burgers and fries and, if I remember correctly, one Cobb salad. And a lot of really interesting conversation. No booogedy-boogedyboogedy, mooooooohawwwwhawwwhawwhawww.

Michael, it turned out, looks kind of like a surfer dude. He's just a regular guy. Well, a regular guy who happens to see ghosts.

That's right, he sees dead people. DEAD PEOPLE! At least the ones who are still hanging around.

He talked about it at lunch in a very matter-of-fact fashion, as if being a psychic was like having a regular office job. The only difference is, instead of looking at a living receptionist and the still-breathing Xerox repairman, he's seeing *dead people*. That's all, he explained.

I asked him about himself first, because the idea of this otherworldly stuff was really quite overwhelming to me. Besides, I have never been one to want to know about the future. I don't know why, maybe it's because I get spooked enough just living in the present. Or maybe it's because I don't want to know when I'm going to die. Whatever the reason, it just freaks me the fuck out. Especially if the person seems to be some sort of seer. Like Michael.

But finally I screwed up the courage and asked Michael how he knew so much about my future.

It turns out the answer was simple. Someone who only Michael could see had told him about me.

He was so earnest when he explained this, I actually believed him. As weird as it sounds, I had the distinct feeling that this was no parlor trick. And I had just had a long lunch with him, so I knew that this was not a stoner with a Ouija board.

For the first time in my life I believed what I had always thought to be false: that there were people with a gift to see into the future. And that Michael was one of them, that it was something he had cultivated, and that he was on the level.

Yes, there was a little part of me that really wanted this tale of a "spectacular career" to be true. Let's face it, being a club comic and staying in a regular room at the Marriott is nice. Being a theater headliner and staying in a suite at the Four Seasons kicks ass. If you ever have the choice, I highly recommend the latter.

Anyway, as my conversation with Michael continued, I learned that his mother had the gift but at first kept it to herself. Then one day she was walking down the supermarket aisle and a woman approached her and told her she knew that she had the gift and that she should stop avoiding it. She should cultivate it.

It was her path. What's more, as time went on, it would be revealed that Michael's entire family—with the exception of his father—also had the gift.

Look, I know you hear these stories all the time. I hear them, too. Sometimes it's an alien who wants to tell a human something important to save the planet. Or it's a human telling an alien which detergent to buy. Or it's just an asshole approaching you to tell you something idiotic because he can't keep his mouth shut.

But this certainly seemed to be legitimate. Well, as legitimate as something that can't be seen or proven can get.

As Michael's story unfolded, I learned that his father was in the army at the time and that this wasn't the kind of thing he was keen on hearing about. Still, his mom continued to meet with the supermarket lady and, eventually, went off with her kids to spend time in a community where others of like mind lived. It was there, in an atmosphere of understanding and acceptance, that she ultimately cultivated her gift.

It brought an end to her marriage. But it also brought out the gift that was in all of her children, including the very young Michael. The newly fatherless family moved to a new home, where, apparently, Michael said there were some hellish spirits already dwelling. He was afraid of them—as who the fuck wouldn't be at his young age? Or, for that matter, at any age? It's got to be disconcerting to see ghouls that the rest of your playground pals don't see at all. And by ghouls I mean ghosts that are in flames—screaming, their faces contorted, a bunch of Caspers on a bad bunch of steroids. The secret to dealing with them, I was told, was to show no fear. Well, good luck with that!

Eventually young Michael summoned his courage and overcame his own fears and learned to live and move easily among the unseen. He told me about this as if he were reciting the multiplication tables or the alphabet. It sure isn't government work—unless, of course, you work in Dick Cheney's office. He may not be dead yet, but he's the scariest ghoul I've ever seen.

Michael now makes his living as a psychic. He gives readings and clears homes of unwanted ghosts. My favorite of his stories is when a young man called to have his house cleared of a female demon that he was having sex with.

Such a demon is called a succubus. Personally, I call it a lucky break. Imagine, a ghost who fucks you. No dinner and drinks or a movie, just sex with a demon. It sounds pretty good. They should advertise certain apartments that way: "Two bedroom, spa bath, fireplace. Succubus included." Where do I sign up? Hey, who wouldn't want to have sex with a ghost? I mean at least once. Just to see what it's like.

According to Michael, this guy did want to give it a try—and, apparently, he did it a lot more than just once. Making matters worse, the succubus had become attached to him, which happens because, well, succubi have feelings, too. So when he started seeing a real live woman, the succubus was *pissed*. And she wasn't shy about showing it. She'd throw shit at this woman. Slam doors in her face. In general, torture her.

Imagine what the living girlfriend was thinking. And, as the guy, what do you say to her to help her to understand? "Hey, baby, I was lonely, she was lonely... So I hooked up with this ghost. Sweetie, it happens."

(And just out of curiosity: If you fuck a succubus, is that adultery? If a blow job isn't sex—as many people feel, including a former president who will remain nameless but is married to a woman named Hillary—then is fucking someone who isn't there a bad thing? It can't be counted against you. Or can it? I'll have to check with some experts on that.)

So how do you get rid of a jealous succubus? According to Michael, you talk to her. You reason with her. You tell her to move the fuck on. And that's just what he did.

I told Michael that the next time something like this came up, he should give the succubus my phone number and address. With me, it's all about giving.

Since I met Michael, he has called me out of the blue a few times, as if he knows full well what is happening in my life. A few years ago as I was literally walking out the door of my apartment, on my way to Los Angeles to shoot a pilot for CBS, the phone rings. It's Michael. He tells me that he knows that I'm going off to shoot my TV show and that I shouldn't sweat it as it's going to go well, and even if it doesn't make the schedule, not to worry, more is on the way.

I can't imagine, knowing Michael as I do, that he's tracked my career development online. And as I had no website then that announced what I was doing, the explanation I keep coming back to is that he just knew. One of his ghost secretaries must have told him.

It was a hell of a nice call to get, just to know that the spirit world is keeping an eye on my career.

Even more amazing, I came home one night after a discussion with friends over dinner about whether or not I would ever have children. I said it would be nice to have a relationship with a woman who might carry my child to term. On the other hand, I also admitted to my friends that I felt I was already too old to have children. A number of people argue this point with me, but I am not one who believes a kid wants to play catch with a seventy-year-old dad. I am not even sure this seventy-year-old dad, with the lifestyle I have led, wouldn't hurt himself playing catch. I am, however, pretty sure my sperm is in such bad shape that my baby would be born with a helmet. Besides, I concluded, I seem to be married to my career, so a wife and child are not really in the cards for me.

It turns out that while I was having this discussion with my friends at a restaurant, Michael left a message for me at home saying I shouldn't dismiss the idea of having children. That it just might work for me. It was as if he had been sitting with us.

Now, whether or not I believe what Michael said, I was stunned. And this was not the first time such a thing had happened with Michael. At our first meeting, Michael said something that truly changed the way I thought about psychics.

He spoke to me about my brother's cancer.

It was like getting hit by a bus.

I remember sitting there, trying to catch what little breath

I had left. There was no way in hell Michael could have known about my brother's condition. Ron had been diagnosed with cancer only a few months before. The diagnosis was not good, though Ron spoke as if it was under control and felt that a cure was imminent. I don't know if that's just what Ron was telling us or if the doctors really felt confident, but Michael alerted me to the fact that my brother's condition was more serious than I was being led to believe.

This information was an absolute eye-opener and it made me more attentive to my brother and his needs.

In light of that, I probably should have done more to help my brother. I certainly should have looked into alternatives to the traditional treatments my brother was receiving. But I did what I could at the time, and as I have learned, you can always do more—you just can't ever do enough. Michael helped me understand that lesson, and I can never thank him enough for being so fearless as to share his amazing abilities and that heartbreaking information with me.

About a year after my brother passed away, I visited Michael again. We sat around his house. He told me that Ron was there with us, which seemed to confirm what I had been feeling—that Ron was always around. Michael said that Ron wanted me to do movies. Hell, he wasn't alone there. I certainly wanted to do movies as well. Michael said I would be doing movies. And a few years later, I was doing movies.

One thing you should know about psychics: They are never

quite sure about the timing. In my dealings with Michael, he is pretty right on about what's going to happen to me. He just can't say if it will happen in October or May, or even in two years. Oh well. We take what we can.

Still, my experiences with Michael have certainly changed the way I look at the world I can't see. To paraphrase Shakespeare, I had begun to learn that there were more things in heaven and earth than I was dreaming of in my philosophy. I found all of this very comforting, much more so than Judaism ever was for me.

Maybe I am crazy. Maybe Michael's crazy. But maybe—just maybe—we are both as sane as can be. That's what I like to think, anyway.

Oh, by the way, for those of you who are wondering: I have never paid Michael a dime. He is my friend—a friend with an extraordinary gift.

it's in the stars

I nearly flunked astronomy in college. And it wasn't my fault. The stars lined up and conspired against me (in a manner of speaking).

I used to go to the Morehead Planetarium on the campus of the University of North Carolina for the lab session of the class. It was from two to four in the afternoon. Once we were seated in the vast hall, they would turn off the lights and the night sky would appear above our heads. That's when my professor's gentle voice, filled with years of terminal boredom brought on by a repetition of facts that he no longer found of much interest, wafted through the air like the sound of crickets. I would fall asleep within minutes.

If memory serves me correctly, the only time I remained awake in this particular class was when a lovely young lass and I diddled each other's fancy in the dark. These moments gave me a deeper appreciation of anatomy, but it did nothing to pique my interest in astronomy.

Besides, it's hard to feel the magic of the night sky when you are wearing glasses that are as thick as mine. "Did you see the shooting star, Lewis?" Who were they kidding? I could barely see Orion's belt. For that matter, I could barely see my own belt.

It should come as no shock when I tell you that I have little interest in astronomy. The same goes for its questionably magical and marginally spiritual cousin, astrology.

I get the genesis of the whole thing. The sky is so vast and so majestically beautiful, why wouldn't one create a mythology to explain it? It sounds logical, but I certainly never thought astrology had any real practical application.

I put about as much stock in it as I do in the practice of voodoo. I am sure it works on some vague level, but not enough for me. (If there is a reader out there who practices voodoo, however, I beg that you don't try to prove me wrong. Especially by putting some wicky-wicky spell on me. If it works for you, I concede I will trust you on this.)

That said, I have to admit that I once had a very strange encounter with the world of astrology. I was wandering around a drugstore in New Haven when an astrology booklet on the magazine rack caught my eye. It was titled *The Love Life of the Virgo*, or some such nonsense, and was written by Sydney Omarr, one of the more well-known and popular astrologers at the time.

I was just coming out of a divorce, so I knew I could use

any advice I could get my hands on. Even advice I thought had no basis in reality. So, since I was born under the sign of Virgo, I figured I'd leaf through the booklet. Couldn't hurt, I thought.

Seeing how my ex-wife was a Leo, I immediately looked up the romantic compatibility of that sign with Virgos. Here's where my eyes popped out of my head. The booklet said the coupling of those two signs would create a rocky union but that under absolutely no circumstances should a Virgo marry a Leo born on either July 23 or July 24. This would lead to disaster.

BING-FUCKING-O!

My ex-wife was born on one of those days. Coincidence? My dick.

This was way too much of a nail-on-the-head sort of shit for me. The booklet was dead on.

As you no doubt have surmised by now, mine wasn't a good marriage. It lasted less than a year.

Okay, so let's do the math. There are three hundred and sixty-five days in a year, and Sydney Omarr—with his charts and graphs and whatever—nails one of the two days that my wife shouldn't be born on. What are the odds? That is more than dumb luck. That's unbelievable.

Perhaps the stars do know something of our fate. Or, perhaps, Sydney Omarr simply knew my ex-wife. Maybe if I'd looked at *The Love Life of the Aquarian* and *The Love Life of the Gemini* that day they also would have warned off marrying anyone born on July 23 or 24. Maybe Syd was just hedging his bet.

Either way, it's things like this that have given me pause, and even a nudge toward some kind of faith in something. I haven't sought out astrologers since then, but I read my horoscope every day. You never know.

And while I've had no revelations as extraordinary as that first one, I guess it's just a reminder that I don't know everything. And neither does my shrink. So maybe from time to time I should listen to the stars.

a call from norman lear

A few years ago I met Norman Lear and his son at the Aspen comedy festival, which was a thrill for me, as he is a hero of mine. He was the creator of some of the finest television comedy ever produced and some of the most intelligent. His work was not only funny, it was often groundbreaking and at times profound.

His *All in the Family* told the tale of Archie Bunker, a lovable bigot who was in a constant battle with the changing world around him and his daughter and son-in-law, who lived under his roof. Norman used this character to confront all sorts of issues that were rarely discussed on television, even on the news or in any other public forum. Racism, sexism, war, women's liberation, and homophobia were all fodder for his satiric wit.

He came up after seeing my act, and I tried to control the voice screaming in my head, "IT'S NORMAN LEAR! IT'SNORMANLEAR!IT'SNORMANLEAR! This happens when I meet people I truly admire.

He told me how much he and his son enjoyed my comedy. And I tried not to jump up and down.

One day a few months later, the phone rang.

"Hello, Lewis, this is Norman Lear."

This is it, I thought. *Finally the breakthrough I have been waiting for.* He had some brilliant TV project he was working on and I would be perfect for it. I will be the new Archie Bunker. I will be the new Maude. I will cork up and be the new Sanford.

I wanted to scream: "YES! FUCK, WHATEVER IT IS I'LL DO IT."

Instead, in as calm a voice as I could muster when talking to a creative legend, I said, "Hi, Norman, how are you doing?"

"I am fine," he said. "I have kind of an unusual request for you. I don't know if anyone has ever asked you to do something like this, but" (YES! FUCK, WHATEVER IT IS I'LL DO IT! echoed through my brain) "would you perform at my son's bar mitzvah? You met him at Aspen. He is a huge fan of yours. You are his favorite comic, and the present that he wants the most is for you to perform at his bar mitzvah."

That, in a nutshell, is the story of my career. Norman Lear finally calls and it's to perform at his son's bar mitzvah. Adam Sandler did *The Wedding Singer,* and it was a huge hit on the big screen. I get reality, not even a reality show.

And then Norman asked: "Have you ever done a bar mitzvah? What's the going rate?"

What's the going rate for my doing a bar mitzvah? *How about a television pilot?* I thought. *Should I call my agent and have him negotiate?*

Of course not. I had no going rate for doing a bar mitzvah. So I just said yes. I did Norman Lear's son's bar mitzvah. No one, anywhere on the planet, has that on their résumé.

Sure, Mr. Pacino, you did *Godfather I, II,* and *III,* but did you ever perform at a bar mitzvah? No, I didn't think so.

So why did I agree to perform at Norman Lear's son's bar mitzvah? Just to say that I did it. That's why. And because Norman is someone I respect and admire and because his son is a terrific kid. Hey, I was his favorite comic, and I was his present. You can't say no to that. How many times outside of a high-security prison are you somebody's present? I wish Bob Newhart had performed at my bar mitzvah.

Oh, and I needed the gig. Seriously. And the money was good—much better than I was making at the time.

It was a good gig, but definitely a strange one. I took the stage where the band had been playing, and the bar mitzvah boy and his friends all crowded in front of me on the dance floor while the adults sat off to my right. I was entertaining a group of thirteen-year-olds.

So I cleaned up my act and forged ahead. I even dusted off some of my Jewish material that I hadn't used in years.

The crowd enjoyed themselves. But I didn't kill. I don't think you can kill at a bar mitzvah.

bo and peep

Religion is supposed to provide solace. Why, then, do so many people who practice religion end up killing themselves?

It's a question that has been nagging at me for some time. Perhaps it's the feeling of failure that overwhelms them when they can't measure up to the kind of life they were told they should be living. And, coupled with either a chemical glitch in their makeup or an overzealous religious leader, they decide to end it all.

Or maybe they are opting for the promise of an eternal life they believe will be so much better than the vale of tears they are forced to endure in this world that they design their own demise. No one knows the body count for sure, but I would hasten to guess the numbers are up there.

Adding to those totals are the religious groups where a number of people make the choice together. The suicide pact orchestrated by Jim Jones immediately comes to mind.

A total megalomaniac psychopath, Jones took a thousand members of his Peoples Temple flock from San Francisco to a life in Guyana. There, he convinced them all to drink cyanide-laced Flavor Aid in 1978, resulting in one of the largest mass suicides in recorded history. And this was a church that was considered extremely progressive and extraordinarily integrated—proving that it is not just the ignorant out there who are capable of displaying extraordinary stupidity.

Now, before I go on, I want to clear something up. Back in '78, Kool-Aid got a very bad rap; it was referred to as the drink of choice at the Peoples Temple that day. That's because nobody had heard of Flavor Aid, which, if truth be told, actually competes with Kool-Aid. Hence the confusion. But now that you know, please don't make that mistake again.

Another group that caught the world's attention was a semireligious one with overtones of alien fantasy called Heaven's Gate. They were by far my favorite. They were the best. Why? They were homegrown! Nobody grows nut jobs with the same panache as the good old U.S. of A.

To begin with, their leader was Bo and his partner was Peep. Go ahead, look it up—it's in the public record. They were Bo and Peep. And they went around the country holding meetings in order to increase their flock.

I don't know about you, but if I was at a meeting and the guy in charge said, "My name is Bo, and this is Peep," that would be the end of the meeting for me. I'd be out of there.

Only one of two things would have kept me there. Either they would have had to be sheep, or Peep would have needed to be dressed appropriately. And that means complete with a bonnet. Most definitely—the bonnet would be very important. If either of those things had happened, they would have had my complete attention.

Well, thirty-nine other Americans didn't have as many rules as I had, and they agreed to follow Bo. And where were they going? To a mother ship which was conveniently located out of sight, right behind the Hale-Bopp comet.

And just how were they supposed to get to the mother ship? Well, according to Bo, the rules were simple. "You don't drink, you don't smoke, you don't do drugs, and you don't have sex."

Well, kill me now. If you are going to take away all four of the major food groups, there is no reason for me to stay around.

Bo and Peep also apparently told their male followers that if they still had sexual urges, they should alleviate them by castrating themselves.

As crazy as that directive sounds, I found references to six disciples—count 'em, six—who chose to be castrated. Call me silly, but castration would be a definite deal breaker. If you found yourself in the bathroom, gripping a weed whacker in one hand and your balls in the other, don't you think you'd hear a little voice cry out, "Hey, hey, hey, I don't think this is the group for us—isn't there a book club in the neighborhood?"

It's not a choice I would have made. Ditto for the choice the group made in 1997 when they chose to kill themselves. En masse. And in a mansion, no less.

The mansion thing, incidentally, was one of the reasons it was all so shocking to most of us. You just don't kill yourself in a mansion—you kill yourself in a leaky tenement apartment with a rusty tub in the bathroom. I know, because I've lived in a lot of places like that in New York, and, trust me, those thoughts go through your head frequently.

But where did these people get the money for a mansion? How could people who had so little contact with reality raise the cash to rent a mansion? Wait, I take that back. Money has always been attracted to a good bogus religion. Besides, it makes it easier when you know you don't have to come up with next month's rent because you're breaking your lease in a huge way.

It should be noted that all the members of this group were wearing Nike sneakers when they died. That was the one thing about this tragic incident that made any sense to me. After all, if you're going to be wearing the same shoes for all eternity, you really want to be sure you're shod in attractive and comfortable athletic footwear. What I do find surprising, however, is that Nike never used this particular ringing endorsement in any of its ads.

Finally, just a word to the wise: When your religion leads you to contemplate taking your own life—the only one you are positive you're going to have—then it's not a religion anymore. It's a death trip.

the god lists:
god the father/god the bother

Reasons I Believe in God

1. Food—especially barbecue, burgers, steak, pasta, cheese, sausage, sausage gravy (I could go on)—and the pill that lowers cholesterol.
2. A perfect martini and a good glass of wine.
3. Seventy degrees, sunny, and a slight breeze.
4. A hole in one. (I actually have had one, and it almost made me believe in Jesus, too.)
5. An airplane taking off and landing on time.
6. A politician who tells the truth.
7. An unexpected check.
8. A dentist who uses nitrous.
9. Actually, *just* the nitrous.
10. Driving across country and one of my favorite songs comes on the radio.
11. Health insurance that actually pays a doctor's bill.
12. A superior massage.
13. A very happy ending.
14. The laughter of a child—in the distance, and never on a plane.
15. Dessert (except Jell-O).
16. The fact that my mother doesn't believe in God.
17. Sleep.
18. Naps.

19. Ireland, Italy, Paris, Chapel Hill, the Berkshires, the Smokies, the Pacific Northwest, and Canada. (Yes, Canada. I am glad it's so close, in case I ever need to move there.)
20. The female breast, of any size or shape. They are not only all perfect, they are also a milk delivery system. (Now, if they used this argument when discussing "intelligent design," I might just listen to those idiots.)
21. To hedge my bets.

Reasons I Don't Believe in God

1. Ticks.
2. *E. coli.*
3. AIDS.
4. Cancer—both the disease and the sign.
5. Crabs.
6. The laughter of a child—especially up close and/or on a plane.
7. Fat.
8. Hemorrhoids.
9. Having to masturbate.
10. The knowledge that someday I won't be able to.
11. *American Idol.*
12. Democrats and Republicans.
13. Anyone who tries to convert me.
14. Herpes.
15. A colonoscopy.
16. The death of my brother.
17. Beets.
18. Catheters.
19. The histories of organized religions.
20. Nazis.
21. The fact that He refuses to reveal Himself to me. But since He doesn't exist, He can't. Right?
22. Because there's doubt.

the whole truth and nothing but the truth, so help me god

Is the Bible absolutely true? Is it truly the word of God?

Well, if it is, I am fucked. And then I'm fucked for saying fuck. And I say it a lot. It's not really a word to me, it's a comma.

It just takes an awful lot of faith to believe that God actually picked out some true believers to tell his story to. After all, we know he didn't write the Bible himself, so it only stands to reason that his book is really the work of middlemen.

But what if the ghostwriters got it all wrong? What if they didn't understand God's nuanced thinking? For all we really know, coveting your neighbor's wife is actually a good thing.

But, even if the Bible is a dead-on accurate transcription of God's words, it's rather shocking that God only had two books in him, the Old and the New Testament. I've actually written two books and I am sure God would have written more than me.

Two books? That was all he had to say to us? You think he would have put out at least a pamphlet in response to the Holocaust. And if not a pamphlet, a couple of well-placed fireballs, for crying out loud. This is the Supreme Being we're talking about, who whacks Sodom and Gomorrah and turns Lot's wife to salt, and Hitler doesn't get so much as a twisted ankle?

It seems a little suspicious to me.

If you believe that God was so involved thousands of years ago with everything happening in the world he created, why did he get tired of his plaything? Perhaps he just lost interest after we supposedly got civilized. Or maybe he's just too busy laughing at us.

Of course there are only a chosen few who could answer that question, seeing how he has only spoken directly to a handful of people. And they are mostly dead. There was Abraham, Isaac, Jacob, Moses, David, and a couple of others along the way. The only living conduit, if we're going to believe him, is the self-proclaimed God talker, Bush the Younger.

Even if we believed at the time that Bush was talking to God while in the White House, I suspect that George Jr.'s short attention span kept him from picking up God's whole message.

"Uhhhhhm, George, are you awake? Do you have a minute? Now try and pay attention. I know it's hard. I had you elected president, as you know, and, as you have told your people in oh so many words, you are the instrument of my will. And you should feel pretty good about that. It came down to you or the trumpet, and, well, those things are just way too noisy.

"But, George, you have to focus here. This is kind of important. I know you feel that Saddam was a very bad man—and he was, you are right about that. And I know you wanted to go after him, but the guy you really want to get is Osama Bin Laden. He's the target. Could you repeat that so I know you got the message? George? George?"

My theory is that Bush the Younger got distracted because he was relishing the pie he was eating and missed the bit about Osama Bin Laden.

You can't blame him. It's hard to concentrate when you are listening to the Lord. It takes a lot of energy. And both Osama and Saddam have an "s" and an "a" in their names. And while God is really important, boy oh boy, so is pie.

But more than the messenger, I have huge problems with the Bible's message. I have talked about this before—even written about it—but I can't say enough about the incredible idea that the world was created in SIX days. And people believe it because it is written in the Bible.

They are even building museums in support of this idea. There's the Big Valley Creation Science Museum in Alberta, Canada, and the twenty-seven-million-dollar Creation Museum in Petersburg, Kentucky. According to the fine folks who run this museum, apparently dinosaurs were created on the sixth day and were on the ark. In fact both museums present evidence that men and dinosaurs lived at the same time, and both offer visual proof of dinosaurs on the ark. Praise the Lord. Now *there's* a summer vacation waiting to happen.

There is also a monthly magazine called *Answers,* with a website—and please hold on to your hats—www.Answersingenesis.org. Even the World Wide Web is being used to proclaim and uphold the truth and authority of the Bible. Around the world—twenty-four hours a day, seven days a week.

I am running out of energy to continue to grace this type of Neanderthal thought with an argument. I really do try to be respectful toward the faith of others, but when it is so completely misguided, it becomes impossible. Still, I will say this as calmly as I can, as calmly and as reasonably as I can, and I think you will admire my restraint:

SCIENCE IS NOT FUCKING VOODOO! SCIENCE IS NOT IN CONFLICT WITH THE LORD ALMIGHTY! IT IS NOT THE WORK OF THE DEVIL!

And while we're on the subject, I'd like to point out—for the benefit of all of the religious naysayers out there—carbon dating is real. It can help us tell how old something is. It can place things in time. THIS SHIT ISN'T MADE UP! You can carbon-date an object and it gives you a sense of how old it is because of the carbon in it. No one is making these numbers up. It's not mumbo jumbo.

THE EARTH IS OLDER THAN SIX THOUSAND YEARS, SO TOUGHSKI SHITSKI!

I would really like to believe that the world was created in six days, but the problem is that I *think*. And nothing fucks up faith more than a good thought.

I should calm down. I know I am not going to change anyone's mind with this approach. But what approach should I use? How do you convince someone who believes, for instance, that the story of Noah is absolutely true and that every single species of known animal fit on a boat and that it was no sweat, because God does those kinds of things?

Look, I believe in miracles as much as the next jaded fuck. I believe they are real. But let's get really real here. If we accept the whole ark story, are we also to believe that there will be some giant fucking spaceship that a future Noah launches in search of another planet when this one is a piece of shit? Let's face it, many people today believe there are only a finite number of years left before the end and therefore they don't give a rat's ass about what we are doing to the environment. I will admit, I can see half of this equation happening. I just don't see the spaceship.

Still, I realize that Noah-like stories comfort people, but so do fairy tales. People just don't base their lives on them. When was the last time you lived platonically with seven dwarves in the woods? I rest my case.

But here is my most compelling argument about why you can't take the Bible at face value. The fact of the matter is that the biblical creation story is written in the Old Testament, and as much as people want to believe that this is the word of God, it is still a book written, undeniably, by the Jewish people. And if anyone knows anything about the Jewish people they know that what we are really good at is the art of bullshitting.

So good at it, in fact, that we were a nomadic people wandering through the desert, convincing other people that we were really an agricultural economy. As I've been trying to tell you, we are really good storytellers.

And that's what the Bible's creation story is, a wonderful story told to people wandering around in a pounding sun and intense heat, to distract them from the fact that they had no air-conditioning. It all boils down to this: One side of this argument is nuts. And not that I'm choosing sides here, but I believe evolution is an important thread in the larger tapestry I like to call reality.

So why does this make me so angry? Fossils! Fossils! Fossils! For God's sake we run our cars on "fossil" fuel. That's it—the argument is over. Game, set, match!

One of the first places I started talking about all of this in my act was Atlanta, Georgia. Looking back on it, what was I thinking? Obviously I wasn't.

After I finished performing, a born-again Christian—who happened to be a very sweet man—approached me.

"Lewis," he said, "you are mistaken. Fossils, my friend, are the handiwork of the devil."

How good is that? Who knew that the devil had a factory where he made millions of fossils, which his minions distributed throughout the earth, in order to confuse my tiny Jewish brain?

I think these completely different ways of looking at the birth of the world have created incredible problems for our country. They are two diametrically opposed views of reality, and they can't both make sense.

I say we all start again—from scratch. I am willing to give up my belief in evolution if they'll give up their belief in a seven-day fast-food concept of creation. If not, I'll stick to my belief that we started out in a slime pool. And I'll take fries with that.

In the early 1980s I wrote the following for the short-lived Mole, *one of the countless attempts at a magazine devoted to political satire. This should give you a good idea of how I felt even then about the belief that the world was created in seven days. It's an updated version of the tale told in Genesis, and it's certainly just as true.*

punk creationism

In the beginning there was a void. We are talking nothing. Zip, zilch, squat, kadingus, nada. It was very slow. And so God, who up to that point had been somewhere else, arrived. In order to get His bearings, He called for a little light. "That's better," said the Lord. Then he divided the light from the darkness so that one day we might have television. He finally called the light day, and the darkness He called night.

The next morning the Lord created beachfront property, the golf courses, and hors d'oeuvres. Hot and cold. And that was the second day. Not what He expected, but it was a start.

The next day He brought forth grass... and other controlled substances (Valium, Thorazine, acid, and cocaine, each after and for its own kind). And then He brought forth the franchises where one might stop for a bite and never know that one had eaten. He created the processing plant, too. God saw that it was a good investment. So that third evening He slept better.

After brunch on the fourth day God made the sun, the moon, and the stars. Hollywood and Vine came as an afterthought. Then He passed out, because He had forgotten His tanning butter.

And on the fifth day He filled the seas with great whales and baby seals to be clubbed. Birds and bees He created so that man would have a sexual role model. He built the condos on every coastline, too. He ate out that night.

The sixth day God awoke after a wet dream but He was not ashamed. He had accidentally made a man and a woman in His own image. And God blessed them and said be fruitful and multiply so that there will never be a need for kiddie porn. And God saw all that He had done; and behold, it gave Him a migraine.

So on the seventh day the Lord created the Sun Belt and the chaise lounge and He retired.

in the land of seagulls and gingham

I haven't had a lot of contact with the Mormon Church, or, as they call themselves, the Church of Jesus Christ of Latter-day Saints. Sure, I remember Donny and Marie from their seventies variety show. I knew one of them was a little bit country and the other one was a little bit rock and roll and together they were nothing less than horrifying as they created the musical equivalent of nausea, but those were TV Mormons, and they therefore never seemed that real to me. I even went to high school in Maryland with a few members of the Mormon Church, but I think they knew better than to try to convert me.

And the Mormons are BIG on converting folks. They send out their young men for two years of missionary work. As a result, at this writing, they are one of the fastest-growing religions on the planet.

I don't understand the appeal myself. But what do I know? Maybe they give out free health-club memberships. Or, more likely, they are growing by leaps and bounds because a church member can convert a dead person to Mormonism.

I will repeat that. Mormons convert dead people.

That's right, they believe that they convert people who aren't alive anymore. I guess they figure if the dead can vote in Chicago, the dead can also change their minds about the religion they no longer practice.

Imagine you're wandering around heaven and you get called to the supervising angel's office and are told you are now a Mormon.

"But I'm a Jew," you might argue.

"No," you are told, "take off the skullcap. The Mormons just drafted you."

The one Mormon I actually spent time with was a guy named Richie. I first met him in Little League, where he was a hell of a fastball pitcher. I couldn't hit that thing for shit. He's the one who made me realize that my career wouldn't be in baseball.

Later, when we were in high school together, he invited a bunch of us to play basketball at his church. I thought he was going to use it to pitch the Mormon way to me, but he didn't. He did, however, run the spiel by my friend Ray, complete with Book of Mormon tableaux featuring Joseph Smith, Brigham Young, and the always good-looking Mr. Jesus Christ.

This poor man's multimedia experience did little to move Ray. Maybe he sat through the lecture so we would have a place to play basketball.

As it turned out, the building was quite an interesting place, as the church's sanctuary actually turned into a basketball court. Which, if I were truly crazy for basketball, might have been reason enough to convert. But, impressive as I find multitasking architecture, I wasn't ready to attend services there on Sunday. It did, however, give us a place to go on Thursday nights, which was nice.

The Mormons certainly know about interesting edifices. They were responsible for one of the more extraordinary sights one could see in my homeland of suburban Maryland. In 1974, they built, in Kensington, a massive white temple with a golden man blowing a huge horn at the top of it. So as you drove the Beltway, it appeared in the distance like a Mormon version of Fantasyland.

This temple was also one of the places a married couple in very good standing in the church could go and, in a room I imagine just like the Hall of Mirrors at Versailles, be married for eternity. This seems like a hell of a gamble to me—50 percent of all marriages in the U.S. barely survive here on earth, and the Mormons are pushing for forever and ever amen. With all the souls dwelling in eternity, isn't it more than possible that you might actually find a better soul mate there, or at least a change of pace? And who knows? Maybe God allows polygamy in heaven.

Speaking as someone who was once married for about five minutes—which certainly felt like an eternity—the concept of being married forever makes my heart stop. Wouldn't you just get slightly sick of your partner after, say, six or seven hundred years? I know I did.

My parents have been married for sixty-five years, and as far as I can tell, the only reason they accomplished this remarkable feat is that they can't hear each other.

Now, before I forget, I want to take a moment to thank the Marriott family, an extremely prominent and successful Mormon clan. They are the owners of the hotel chain bearing their family name. They also used to run a chain of restaurants called the Hot Shoppes, one of which was conveniently located near where I grew up, and my high school friends and I would gather there after running amok on Saturday nights. It is there that I learned the consummate joy of a plate of french fries with gravy. It was my first sense of what, on a very basic level, could be called gourmet food. It was a completely fulfilling and transcendent experience. If, at the time, I had known this was the creation of a Mormon family, I would have been a lot more receptive to their religious pitch, as long as the fries and gravy kept coming.

Of course, that was back in the day. Now it would take a lot more than a potato product au jus to pique my interest. Let me explain.

Not too long ago, I spent ten weeks shooting a movie in Salt Lake City, Utah, the Vatican of the Mormon religion. It's not what I would call a vacation kind of town, especially if you like a bit of a drink every now and then, and who doesn't during a vacation? Still, if you are thinking about visiting there, remember that it's a big wide wonderful world and you might want to save Salt Lake City for last. Like after you've already toured Afghanistan and Iraq. I'm talking about when you are in your late eighties and you have seen everywhere else.

Read that again. Everywhere.

But back to the ten weeks I spent there. With a little due diligence, you can actually find a cocktail.

For instance, if you want to drink at a bar, first you have to pay an entrance fee to go in. I have no idea why; maybe it's some kind of state law. I would ask every time I paid, but I wasn't told anything that made any sense to me. It's the Mormon way, I guess. Once you finally get into the bar, the bartenders don't even serve you a legitimate shot. It's a little less than a shot; my guess, it's a Mormon shot.

What's more, you can't get a real drink—and by real drink I mean a double. Instead, you have to order what used to be called a sidecar—a short shot in another glass, and you have to pour it in yourself. I guess because that's the way Jesus would do it.

And God forbid if you order a martini. The olive is always higher than the gin or vodka, depending on your pleasure. And I'm talking a regular-sized olive here—your standard olive from a jar—not some mutant Mormon creation.

One of the more sobering moments I had while in this

land of Mormons was with a young Indian woman (as in the country, not Native American). She drove me to the set the first day of shooting and told me she was going to school at Brigham Young University, where she was majoring in film.

Wow, I thought, she must be a Mormon. I had never heard of anyone attending that particular university because of its film school. UCLA and NYU, yes. Brigham Young, not so much. I asked if she was, in fact, a Mormon. She said yes.

I just had to ask, "Are your parents Mormon as well?"

"Oh, no," she replied.

I was stunned. How does one go from the background of an Indian culture of Hinduism or Islam, so clearly non-Christian (they don't even have potluck suppers) to the all-Americanism of the Church of Jesus Christ of Latter-day Saints? She said her parents allowed her to examine all religions and to find one that appealed to her. She chose to become a Mormon. She told me if I found that odd, her brother had chosen to join the Jews for Jesus.

The conversation rendered me speechless, a condition I rarely find myself in. I wanted to say something. I just had no idea where to start.

Compared to her brother's, her choice almost looked like a smart one. And it makes you wonder what her folks are like. I wanted to ask her about them, but my brain wasn't up to the task. I did, however, have the wherewithal to ask her to drive me to the big church in town.

If you do ever find yourself in Salt Lake City, I suggest you take the tour of the Mormon Tabernacle. If you are going to be in a city run by Mormons, it's good to know what they are up to.

On the day I was there, there were about twenty of us on the tour and we were led by a young girl in a gingham dress. This was quite exciting, because you don't see gingham anywhere anymore—unless you spend all of your free time at craft fairs.

On the tour, we saw the actual first Mormon temple built in Salt Lake City in the 1800s, entirely out of granite. The guide explained how far away the granite quarry was and how hard it was to get the stone overland and that it took forty years to complete. I half-expected to hear her say that three thousand Jews died in the process, but she never said anything about that.

You rarely find much humor in any religious type of tour.

So there I was, staring up at this extraordinary structure, with its magnificent spires jutting straight into the sky. I was truly overwhelmed by the size of the structure and the hard work and faith of the people who had built it.

That's when it happened. I thought I was thinking it, but I actually said it.

The words "Jesus Christ" came spilling right out of my mouth.

Everyone within earshot turned to look at me, and the

crystal-clear, stone-cold silence of their judgment descended on me like the wrath of God.

This was a huge faux pas in that community. I had blasphemed in their temple. I wanted to stop the young girl in gingham and explain to her that, as a Jew, I wasn't actually taking his name in vain. It was merely an expression of my excitement. And I thought it was a nicer way of expressing what I was really thinking, which was, "Fuck, look at that son of a bitch."

Lesson learned. I should have just said, "Wow!"

At the end of the tour, our group went up a flight of stairs and sat in a semicircle in front of a twelve-foot-tall animatronic Jesus who spoketh unto us-eth. It was a collection of the usual Jesusisms: "Love thy neighbor as thyself"—that type of stuff. I have to say, as a Jew, it's not going to get any better than that. I don't do drugs anymore and I still wanted to spend the whole day with the guy. It was that amazing.

Even on a nonreligious level, it's very weird to have a Chuck E. Cheese Jesus speak to you. It would be like if you were a Catholic and went to Mass on Sunday and the Jesus up on the crucifix turned to you and just started talking. "Hey, how's everyone doing? What a nice crowd, and, may I say, a good-looking one to boot. Remember, it's Bingo Night next Friday, and I know you love that. And don't worry about a thing, I'll be down in a minute." It's kind of fascinating and freaky.

After the tour, I took the young girl in gingham aside and asked her, "Was Jesus really that tall?"

"Metaphorically," was her icy reply. I was amazed she responded at all.

Though if Jesus really was that tall, it would certainly explain Christianity. Back then people were about five foot five, and if there was a twelve-footer around, they were going to follow him everywhere and listen to everything he had to say. I know I would have. Definitely.

If Jesus Christ were to return to earth today and went on the Mormon Tabernacle tour and saw the twelve-foot version of himself, he would probably say, "Turn that off! He doesn't even have my hair color!"

As impressive as the twelve-foot Jesus and the granite temple and even the Mormon Tabernacle Choir, which I have heard on occasion, are, they're not enough to sway me toward the Mormon way. A huge stumbling block for me is the concept of polygamy, which was practiced by the first members of the Church until the rest of the country cracked down on what they considered to be nonsense and contrary to Judeo-Christian principles. A number of sects broke off from the LDS, because they believe it is an important tenet of the Mormon faith. I find it tough to believe that God wants man to be polygamous. I think it takes a guy to come up with that idea. Though how you make a concept like that work is beyond me. Most men aren't equipped to deal with one woman, let alone several at the same time.

If I had to choose between becoming a Latter-day Saint

and accepting the infallibility of the pope, I'd have to go with the pope. I guess for starters, it's just tough for me to believe in a religion with American roots (except for those of the Native Americans). Call me spiritually prejudiced, but the fact is, looking at all the varieties of Christian faith, the Mormons and those Baptists who use rattlesnakes during their service really seem to me to be pushing the envelope.

Besides this, I find it really tough to swallow the story that the founder of the Mormon Church, Joseph Smith, tells—of how the prophet Moroni appeared to him and told him where to find the gold plates, which were buried fourteen hundred years prior to their meeting, and on which was written the text that would become the Book of Mormon. Smith is instructed not to do anything with them yet, but he goes to get them anyway. Lo and behold, the gold plates vanish. Smith says he got greedy. Still, Moroni tells him he'll give him another chance and he should return to the very same spot of their meeting every September 22.

Are you following this so far? I am trying to keep it simple.

So Smith goes back each year and meets Moroni, who tells him what God wants him to do with the plates. But still Moroni doesn't give him a second set. This goes on for three years and then Smith is told that next time, maybe—and it's a big maybe, mind you—he just might get the plates if he does what God wants him to do, which is to marry a young woman that Smith just happens to have the hots for.

Okay, here's where the fun comes in. The young woman's father won't grant his daughter's hand in marriage. Would you? Who wants their daughter to marry a guy like that? But the daughter defies the irate father, and the lovebirds elope.

This seems to do the trick. In 1827, at the age of twenty-one, Smith returns to the spot and Moroni shows up and gives him the plates. Apparently, nineteen folks claimed they saw these plates and eight of them say so at the beginning of the Book of Mormon.

Don't get too comfortable. The story doesn't end there.

Moroni then tells Smith that his next job is to get the text on the plates transcribed onto paper. But since it is written in some kind of Egyptian language, Moroni gives him glasses that will allow him to translate it. (By this point, incidentally, I feel as if I am knee-deep in bullshit.)

So Smith begins to translate the text while his neighbor takes down his dictation. They finish 116 pages and then the neighbor loses the manuscript.

For God's sake, make it end.

Anyway, Moroni had taken the plates and the glasses back, so Joseph had to get him to give those sacred items back to him *again,* even though he has now screwed up for a second time. (It is believed the neighbor's wife threw the manuscript out, and quite frankly who could blame her? This story is a little hard to swallow.)

But Moroni doesn't give him the glasses, so now in order

to get the translation, Smith places a stone in a hat and sticks his head in the hat and puts the plates near the hat.

Finally—big drumroll, please—the words appear in the hat, and by 1829 the translation of the Book of Mormon is complete.

Keep in mind, history tells us that all of this is the work of Joseph Smith, who had been convicted of fraud after being paid to locate buried coins of silver or gold and was unable to do so. Oh, and he was using the same stone, by the way, during that ill-fated incident that he used in his Book of Mormon hat trick. So I think you might see why this sounds a bit far-fetched to me. (You can find a more complete telling of this tale, incidentally, in Jon Krakauer's fantastic *Under the Banner of Heaven*, but I pretty much hit all of the high points.)

Oh, one more thing. According to this translation of plates done by a man staring at a stone in a hat, a large group of Hebrews left Jerusalem and sailed to North America. Eventually they split into two groups; one was white, and one was dark (the dark group being Native Americans). Now each group was led by one of two brothers, the dark one jealous of the white one, because his father had made the lighter guy leader of the tribe.

Then, who should arrive after his Resurrection, but Jesus himself (I guess he was an avid tourist), and he converts them to his teachings. They live in peace for a while, until the darker ones turn their collective back on Jesus and a war breaks out and the dark ones slaughter all the white guys. (This, no doubt, is why blacks weren't allowed to become priests in the Mormon Church until 1978.)

This all seems like nonsense, and it's incomprehensible to me what draws in converts from around the world. It's an all-American religion, and its roots are very, very, very white. There's something Disneyesque about it. I don't know if it's the Fantasyland Temple or the Davy Crockett aspect of crossing the country looking for new frontiers as they were hounded out of settlement after settlement.

All religions require a leap of faith—I'm not saying that Moses' burning bush is any easier to believe than the gold plates—but this one seems to need a rocket pack to make the leap.

The tour of the temple mentions very little of the history of the religion. It's presented as a Christian religion steeped very deeply in traditional family values.

The girl in gingham was one of the happiest people I ever met, and even my unorthodox behavior didn't faze her. Faith can bring a real joy to people, but if you don't believe, then you feel like you're in Oz and you're the only one who doesn't believe in the Wizard.

islam. all i'm saying is, i got nothing to say

I have nothing to say. Nothing. And let's leave it that way.

I am sure there will be some Muslim somewhere who will be upset that I didn't say anything about his faith. That's the funny thing about religion. It doesn't matter what you say, you are going to upset someone.

So do whatever you've got to do and I'll get back to you later, when things have settled down. Go on, pick up the dry cleaning or stop at the post office. I'll wait for you at the next chapter. Really, I'll be fine here.

when bobby goes boom

Over the past few years, religious suicide bombers have been making quite a name for themselves. Which is not surprising—after all, it's hard to forget someone who blows up half a city block because he doesn't like the God everybody else is praying to.

It's got to be a bitch to recruit people for this type of work. Even after an exhaustive national search, what are you going to end up with? Four, maybe five nutcases? I can't think you'd get more than that.

And how do you even start the interview? "Hey, did you ever think about blowing yourself up for your Lord and master? What better way to show him how much of a true believer you are? So, does it sound like something you'd like to do? Trust me, it's the fastest way to become all the billions of bits you can be."

It's the kind of mystery that I fear will be answered only in the afterlife. Which, in the cruelest irony of all, means the suicide bombers will hear it first.

And, sadly, there is a precedent for this kind of deadly aggression. The suicide bombers of today are merely spiritual descendants of the Japanese kamikaze pilots of World War II.

One just wishes the Japanese had taught these latest practitioners of their lethal art a bit of war etiquette. At least in the forties the pilots limited their attacks to the enemy forces they were fighting and not to the enemy's civilian population. Man, it is so depressing to think that those were the good old days.

the suicide bomber's prayer

To begin with, please forgive me for calling you simply the Holy One. I shall not mention your actual name because I am not looking for any trouble from the community that is currently misguidedly working in your name. I figure you'd be cool with that, seeing as you understand everything.

Also, before we get bogged down with the really big stuff, please allow me, in all of your infinite wisdom, to find something funny really soon. As you know, when you are ready to blow yourself to bits for a belief, you are not a big laugher. I might let out a high-pitched hysterical squeal every now and then, but not what I would call a real feel-good, from-the-gut laugh. I beg you for one more guffaw before I die. Hell, I'll even settle for a less hearty tee-hee.

All I ask is for you to throw me a crumb, Holy One.

I also pray to you that brother Hazmat is correct in his assessment of my possibilities after I leave this earth for good. He says that after I perform this task—a task, incidentally, that I have been assured is of the utmost importance to your divine plan—I will meet seventy-two virgins in the afterlife. Is that true? Can you give me a sign or something on that?

My American college friend Brad said that it seemed impossible to him. But like I said, he is an American—and we all know what their women are like. Even his sister. I don't want to tell tales out of school, but I had her.

Oh, sweet Jesus, I just smiled. Hey, thanks for that.

Finally, and this is really important, I pray that brother Blow Shid Ap knows what he is doing with the explosives. Please guide his every move—or those virgins will be worthless to me. Oh, before I forget, thanks for giving me this chance and for giving me something special to do on a Saturday afternoon.

the amish

You've got to love the Amish. You really do. There they are, surrounded by the madness of this country—us with our ever-evolving obsession with technological innovations—and yet somehow are able to stick to their faith and their simple life without batting an eyelash. This is something that I can only view with reverential awe.

How have they managed to do it? And to do it without *bothering* anybody. It's astonishing. Memo to all other religions: Watch and learn. Now.

Who knows if the Amish think we are all sinning as we piss away electricity and every other form of natural and man-made power? Who knows if they think we will fry in a hell where we will spend eternity planting and harvesting without the aid of any motorized farm equipment? Who knows if they even hate us?

They just may. (I know I would.) But they wisely and kindly keep it to themselves. I really like that about them. The radical Islamists could learn a thing or two from our buggy-riding friends.

The Amish are obviously safe in the knowledge of the uprightness of their lives, and they see no need to push it on to anyone else. For God's sake, they even let their children run wild among us, knowing that one day they will return home. And guess what? The vast majority of them do.

Granted, there has been the occasional drug bust, but otherwise you never hear anything bad about the Amish. By and large—and at the risk of mixing metaphors here—these people fly right in a world without a rudder. What's more, they make really terrific and sturdy furniture, grow delicious vegetables, and their chicken is very, very tasty.

I ought to know. There's a comedy club in Lancaster, Pennsylvania, that I played a few times. There isn't much to do except wander around among the Amish farms and stop off and enjoy the fruits of their labors. Do it sometime, if you get the chance. I guarantee you won't be disappointed. (Maybe I should do their travelogue someday.)

I'd become Amish, but I am way too lazy and way too crazy. And I like buttons way too much.

on being a born-again christian

I don't quite grasp the concept of being "born again," in much the same way that I don't get being a Jew for Jesus. The logic just doesn't compute.

Isn't the trauma of being born once really enough for us in this lifetime? And why would you compare the idea of embracing God to birth? I mean, the thought of being expelled from the insulated and regulated comfort of your mother's womb into the blinding glare of harsh light and the crisp, cold air of a sterile delivery room doesn't seem all that appealing to me. Especially if you're going to be covered in blood and amniotic fluid, shrieking and bawling for all the world to hear. For the same effect, you could just watch *Hardball with Chris Matthews*.

Shouldn't they call it something else? Like, It-Was-So-Good-I-Am-Going-to-Do-It-Again Christian? Or maybe a Nouveau Christian? Or how about a Zippity Doodah Christian? That's catchy.

The larger question is: Why, if you are already a Christian, do you need to be born again? If it didn't work the first time, maybe God was telling you something. Face it, how do you know he wasn't? And doesn't it make God suspicious of your commitment to him—to have to do it twice? (I should ask these questions to a born-again Christian, but I'm being rhetorical here.)

And I don't really care why a Jew would be for Jesus, either. Listening to the explanation would render me deaf. And dumb. And really, really pissed off.

the profits

In case you were wondering just how we ended up in the shitter we're now in, I can point it out exactly. It was the moment when the Prophets became the Profits.

There is absolutely no question that since I was born in 1948, the level of greed in this country has grown by leaps and then bounds and then into a fantasy land where it wasn't even real profits, just bubbles bursting into thin air. People couldn't seem to get their hands on enough material wealth to satisfy themselves. They lived their economic lives with less discipline than a crack whore. They had to have a home that was the size of a hotel, and a vacation home in Aspen and another on Turks and Caicos, and an apartment in New York for when they needed to shop for the jewelry that was necessary for the locale they were in at the time. And there were never enough cars, because what if you felt like driving an SUV that day because the Mercedes-Benz Blowjob wasn't blowing you hard enough? And let's not forget the private jet to get everybody to all the places that they never had enough time to spend time at.

Even if you didn't have the money for any of these things, you wanted to cover your ass with a logo or the name of a major designer to show that you knew what good was. Because being good was no longer as important as having the goods.

In a world gone gaga over every new golden calf of conspicuous consumption, where were people who cried "Enough"? Where were our Isaiahs, Ezekiels and Hoseas? (I bet you're shocked I know these names. What do you expect? I wrote a book about religion, for crying out loud.) Where are our Prophets today? Are they screaming their prophesies at the padded walls in their cells at homes for the criminally insane? Or are they mumbling their way down the streets and subway platforms of cities across America with their message of doom for the sinner? Occasionally I will pass a loner on a street corner, Old or New Testament in hand, screaming at the sky about the coming of the apocalypse brought on by our evil ways. This seems to come out of a need for personal redemption, since the financial rewards of this life are out of their reach, as they usually appear to be fucking nuts. But then again, maybe they're our soothsayers, the truly holy who speak the truth. Wouldn't that be a bitch? We're not even listening.

Are the pundits who litter our airwaves or the bloggers who clutter the Internet supposed to be modern-day prophets? If they are, then we are truly fucked, since they're more interested in the sound of their own voice or seeing their words on a computer screen than they are in spreading the truth. Because the only truth to them is their Nielsen rating or the number of hits their website gets.

Do you need to wander a desert to be a prophet? Is that part of the entrance exam? Is that why we have no one in religious communities who seems to deliver divinely inspired revelations? (Unless you count the pope, those who speak in tongues, and the head of the Mormon Church, but I don't. The pope is too concerned with maintaining a lifestyle suitable for the Middle Ages. Those who speak in tongues are incomprehensible. And the head of the Mormon Church is the head of the Mormon Church. I rest my case.)

I've come across four prophets in my life worth paying attention to. They are Bob Dylan, George Carlin, Kurt Vonnegut, and Lenny Bruce. And three of them are dead.

The funny thing is, I don't think any of them would consider themselves Prophets or even prophets with a small *p*. They were just pursuing the truth. And by doing that, they altered the way I looked at the world, thereby making it easier for me to deal with it.

Am I saying that today's seers are found only in CD racks, digital downloads, and bookshelves? Well, maybe. Okay, yes. You take what you can get in this world. And those are four I took. They make me feel less crazy. Their work says to me: "You're not crazy. They are." That really helps.

Maybe other prophets speak to you. If they do, that's okay. I don't have all the answers—and neither do Dylan, Carlin, Vonnegut, and Bruce. (It sounds like a law firm.) What I do know is that telling the truth is hard to do but harder to miss. So when you come across it, pay attention. It does help. And help is better than nothing.

separation of church and statesmen

I have never given a shit what religion the president is. He could worship a can of peas for all I care. I just want him to be good at what we elected him to do, which is to lead the United States of America.

Of course it would be nice if he had a strong moral ethic, but whatever God he wants to worship is of no concern to me. And I couldn't give a shit if he shows up at any given church on any given weekend. Sure, walking into a house of worship has been a publicity mainstay for each and every president since the birth of this nation, but to me it looks like nothing more than a show.

Of course, if the president is going to be *really* religious, it would be nice to know that up front, before we elect him. For instance, it would have been helpful to know that Bush the Younger was going to view himself as God's Hammer. That's the kind of information I consider important.

I guess the lesson that we learned with this administration—

or at least that some of us have learned—is to watch when the son of a bitch keeps blowing the religious horn. Maybe we could have convinced him he would have been happier as a preacher instead of the leader of the free world.

I know I would have been.

he made the blind to walk and the crippled to see

The problem with many religious leaders is that they take a truly wonderful series of ideas about how we should all live together and then refuse to practice what they have so loudly and so annoyingly preached. We all know who I'm talking about, so let's get to it.

My first memories of televangelists come from when I was very young, in the mid-1950s. Now, it always amazes me when people have vivid memories of their early childhoods, like before they were seven, while I can't remember what happened yesterday before seven. But, for some reason, these on-air men and women of God have stuck with me.

I can, as if in a fog, remember a sweating Oral Roberts working in a tent in hopes of converting the masses. The man was working in a *tent*, for God's sake, wandering from village to town, tramping through the Midwest and the South, looking for converts. IN A TENT. Remarkable! Did I mention he had a tent? And he was working without a script or a teleprompter, let alone air-conditioning. The mind reels.

He made a huge impression on me. I was mesmerized, and I was only watching him on TV, so I can't imagine what it must have been like seeing him in person.

I don't recall much of what Roberts actually did or said, just the bombast and the rhetoric. Although I'm pretty sure he threw down a few healings. But most of all I remember the tent.

Since then I've been fascinated by televangelists. Shooting the shit at a spectacular pace, all the while cruising the stage like rock stars, these men and women are spinning their own brand of logical illogic in order to lead their followers to their Lord Jesus Christ—who, it seems, is always standing just a few feet from the collection plate. Screw Streep and De Niro, these guys are some of the finest actors to ever grace our planet.

It's as if they invoke the name of God to maintain their credit line and the lunacy of their devoted followers. And they rewrite all the rules of the game so that they, of course, get to run the nuthouse. And the asylum just seems to get bigger and more crowded all the time.

From those humble beginnings, Roberts went on to build a university in Tulsa, Oklahoma, which he named after himself. I visited it a number of years ago. It has the strangest entrance sculpture of any school on earth: two giant bronze hands in prayer. I guess the buried guy whose hands are coming out of the ground is praying for everyone to get straight A's.

What's more, there's a museum on campus devoted to the

life and works of the Reverend Roberts. You can actually take a tour of his life, and each room is devoted to a representation of a certain period in it. You've got to admire the ego of a guy who would create a full-scale diorama about himself.

Doesn't God at some point say, "Excuse me, but that's a little over-the-top for my taste?" And, come to think of it, shouldn't the museum be devoted to the life of, oh, I don't know, *Jesus Christ*? Really, Reverend Roberts, which of you is more important?

But the most impressive part of the campus is a huge prayer needle where you can call (or now e-mail) what you would like prayed for, and there are sincere, God-loving people on duty 24/7 ready to pray for you. *Ka-ching. Ka-ching.*

In one of my favorite stories about Oral Roberts, a nine-hundred-foot-tall Jesus appears before him and commands him to build a hospital on the campus. Wouldn't you or I just say Jesus appeared to us in a vision? Isn't that sufficient? Doesn't the 894 or so feet Roberts added to his height make him seem—I don't know, I may be jumping to conclusions here—a little nuts?

But the giant Jesus sort of pales in comparison to that other great sales ploy that Roberts pulled off in 1987. I'm referring to when he told his followers that unless he raised eight million bucks, the Lord would call him home. And not to a split-level outside Tulsa, either. No, he was talking about all the way home. You've got to love a guy who mentions God in his ransom note.

Not all evangelists are like Roberts. Billy Graham was cut from a different cloth entirely. He would take his time with the language, bathing each word in an oratory that would have made Lincoln proud. His movement was minimal, for he felt there was no need for a show. As far as he and his followers were concerned, God and his One True Son existed, and simply intoning the words of the Bible was all that was necessary to show the complete and utter proof of His existence.

If there was any emphasis necessary, in fact, he would beat the book, as if to make it sound like thunder from the heavens. Or perhaps he was asking, "How blind are you that you can't see the point that I am making so obviously?" But unlike many of the other televangelists, Billy Graham certainly seemed to be a class act.

He did, however, make a few slipups along the way. Most noticeably, when it came to my Jewish brethren.

Take, for instance, Graham's response to then-president Nixon, who was complaining about Jews and their influence in American life.

"This stranglehold," opined Graham, "has got to be broken or the country's going down the drain."

What a guy.

But Graham did allow that he had some Jewish friends in the media who "swarm around me and are friendly to me."

Talk about a nice image—just like the plague of locusts that descended on Egypt when Pharaoh wouldn't let the Israelites leave.

Graham finally confided to Nixon, "They don't know how I really feel about what they're doing to this country."

When Jewish organizations characterized these quotes as anti-Semitic, Graham defended himself by saying he may have been sucking up to Nixon.

Oh, brother.

I ask you, why would someone who knew God On High feel the need to personally suck up to a guy like Nixon? It certainly sounds like he was working his way down the food chain.

Despite that transgression—or perhaps because of it—Graham was such an icon to his peers that Jim and Tammy Faye Bakker bought Billy Graham's ancestral home and moved it to their Christian village at Heritage USA in Fort Mill, South Carolina. That log cabin (honest—it's a log cabin!) was the first thing you saw when you entered the compound. I know this because I visited there when the Bakkers were at their height.

Jim and Tammy Faye were unusual in many ways. First, they were a duo, while most televangelists fly solo. Also, they worked mainly seated because, I guess, God likes to relax, too.

These two were folksy to the point of absurdity. The only thing their set lacked was a cracker barrel. But as dumb as they may have seemed, they understood the medium of television better than anyone. Oral may have had his tent and Billy his stadiums, but these sly ones worked right out of a television studio built specifically to deliver their message. And their message was achingly simple: Send us money, and then send us more money, and don't forget the MONEY!

They were spectacular in their heyday. They were Burns and Allen on a religious crack pipe, and God was presented like their regular dealer, and as with any dealer, you had to spend a half hour listening to his bullshit with a smile on your face.

The two acted as if they were a happily married couple. The trouble is they were bad actors. Jim Bakker was the exasperated but understanding husband who bantered with Tammy Faye, his daffy wife. It was excruciating and terrifying to watch, like the car wreck you can't take your eyes off of. It usually ended with Jim saying with faked, poorly disguised condescension, "Oh, Tammy." And Tammy would do her part to cue the audience by hysterically giggling over whatever of her hijinks Jim had brought up for the audience's consideration. The studio audience would lap it up, laughing at exchanges that would make me cringe.

When the dialogue wasn't lighthearted, it would turn into a maudlin soap opera based on the travails of their flock or the world at large. Jim would tell a tale of woe about a family without money or a young boy with a malignant brain tumor. Or they'd bring out a drug-addicted, tattooed former biker who had found his way to Jesus after going through one nightmarish experience after another, until, one day, by accident, he stumbled onto their TV show. All the while, Tammy would sob in the background. This would ruin the pounds of makeup she had slapped on before the show began. She wore so much she would have made a Bantu warrior proud. The truth was, you didn't need to do drugs when you watched those two. They *were* the drugs.

Back during the heyday of the Bakkers' PTL Club, a theater in Charlotte, North Carolina, was producing a play I wrote. As luck would have it, the Bakkers were only eighty or so miles away. A macabre fascination drove me to visit. How could anyone pass a thing like that up?

So off we went. The merry scouting party consisted of three people: my girlfriend at the time, Kathy, who was as withering a cynic as I have ever met; my brother, who never passed up a good laugh; and me. We were off to see the Religion of Oz.

After passing the aforementioned log cabin of the Reverend Billy Graham, we were stopped at an entrance where I was sure we would be turned away as unrepentant heathens. I panicked that they might have some sort of Jew detector that would pick up any hint of irony or sarcasm in the area.

It turns out they just wanted to welcome us, tell us where to park, and instruct us on all the diversions that Heritage Village had to offer. It was like a very smiley version of Village of the Damned.

Our first stop was the hotel, where behind the front desk,

in huge letters, was some pious-sounding expression or other like, "Our room service is just another one of God's miracles." We spoke to a guy who was shining shoes, who was happier than I will ever be. He told us how he quit a high-paying job to move there and shine shoes for Christ Almighty. Listening to him, you had to make sure you didn't grind your teeth and spit them out.

We then wandered about the grounds. I think I was traumatized by the experience, as I don't have a clear memory of what we saw. I know for sure, however, that we visited the PTL's version of the Garden of Gethsemane (no joke) and then enjoyed lunch at the Jesus Dined for Our Sins Luncheonette (joke).

I also remember there were all sorts of Christian doodads for sale, such as wall hangings with Bible quotations and skillfully retouched photos of Jim and Tammy.

Later we visited their state-of-the-art television studio, where all of the Christlike magic happened. It was extraordinary. There we were, standing in the very same hallowed hall where they shot their *Praise the Lord Club* television show—or *PTL*, as it was known (much the same way *Saturday Night Live* is called *SNL*, proving once more that comedy rules). We marveled at the fact that when it came to getting out the message, these folks weren't fooling around.

And the money poured in. These fuckers were even selling time-shares in a Christian condo complex. In fact, they were selling more time-shares at this luxury complex than could actually be accommodated. We figured they must have loved the movie *The Producers* so much that Mel Brooks would be given his own wing. Either way, it's a good Christian who makes sure everyone is in on the deal.

We even went to see the homes they were selling. At that time, houses in the area were going for about $50,000, while their little tiny places had price tags of $100,000 and more. To be fair, however, we were told that angels from heaven did all of the yard work.

Jim and Tammy also built a home for a young quadriplegic kid whom they would trot out from time to time to be on the show. Nothing works better than a good cripple to put a whack on the cash cow. You really had to admire the balls of it all. And their balls were so big and brassy they clanged like cathedral bells with every step.

Still, it was amazing to me that Christ hadn't returned to earth to smite these guys. I mean, He and His Father used to smite other folks for a lot less provocation. Face it, God whacked Lot's curious wife after she looked back to see the destruction of Sodom and Gomorrah when God had warned her not to.

The world of televangelists is as competitive as the Yankees–Red Sox rivalry. So this chapter wouldn't be complete without two of the more serious competitors for the Christian dollar, Pat Robertson and Jerry Falwell, the Laurel and Hardy of Christianity.

Jerry passed away while I was writing this book, and I hate to speak ill of the dead, but this guy spoke ill of the living. So here goes.

I was driving down with my family from the D.C. area to Chapel Hill to go to school when I first noticed a small church with a couple of school buses as we passed near Lynchburg, Virginia. Every ensuing time I passed it, something had been added to the place. Another building here, a few more school buses there, a new wing on the church. Over my four undergraduate years at Chapel Hill, I watched as this little church grew into a massive operation.

In addition, Jerry also built a university—and he did it all espousing an extraordinary form of ignorance while invoking the name of Jesus Christ. As if Jesus supported Falwell's petty animosities toward queers and Jews and any other group that wasn't a part of what he saw as the Moral Majority. But when it comes down to it, some of what Jerry had to say wasn't very moral—nor, as far as I could see, did he really have a majority of any sort.

Jerry was one mean, fat man of the cloth. Case in point: Right after September 11, Jerry Falwell said the following: "I really believe that the pagans, and the abortionists, and the feminists, and the gays and the lesbians who are actively trying to make that an alternative lifestyle, the ACLU, People for the American Way, all of them who have tried to secularize America, I point the finger in their face and say, 'You helped this happen.'"

He did this on television, no less—on Pat Robertson's *The*

700 Club. And Robertson agreed with this incredibly insightful analysis.

Jesus Christ, I can't be alone here. I'm of a mind that says you can think whatever nonsense you want to get you through the day, but don't say this kind of stuff out loud. Especially on television. Especially if you are a religious figure.

What was this asshole thinking? Did the Lord have Jerry on speed dial? Did he tell Jerry that these people were responsible for 9/11? He said "pagans"?! Where the hell do you find a pagan nowadays? Let alone a group of them. And I'm not talking your run-of-the-mill heathen here. I mean a really good pagan. It's tough.

And who knew that America's gay and lesbian communities wielded that kind of power? And if they actually have that kind of power, wouldn't they use it to pass laws allowing gay marriage instead of blowing up buildings?

As for feminists, they don't have time for this kind of thing. They are way too busy attending craft fairs. And besides, by September 11, 2001, how many feminists were left? They seem to have moved into the closet vacated by the gays.

The abortionists, meanwhile, have already carved their path to hell, so they don't need to pull a number like this. The ACLU was too busy indirectly defending Falwell's right to spew such bullshit, so the people there couldn't be involved. And the People for the American Way has no power, as it only has nine members.

I've never told anyone this before, but in a very strange twist, after I first read Falwell's statement about 9/11, God called me and said the reason for 9/11 was because He was totally embarrassed by the Reverends Jerry Falwell and Pat Robertson. And despite the havoc and loss He caused, He sounded so contrite that I have to admit I felt a little sorry for Him.

See? Even I can be forgiving.

But back to Falwell. None of what he said should have come as a shock, for this is the same guy who in the late seventies said that "gay folks would just as soon kill you as look at you." The fact that you could say such a thing and not be defrocked is beyond the boundaries of human comprehension. So when the AIDS epidemic hit, Falwell must have been overjoyed; as he said at the time: "AIDS is not just God's punishment for homosexuals; it is God's punishment for the society that tolerates homosexuals."

It actually got worse. He moved out of the vicious into the absurd when he accused one of the Teletubbies of being gay.

Someone should have taken Jerry in for counseling.

First off, what was he doing watching this unbearable show for preschoolers, anyway? And second, how did he figure that a costumed character named Tinky Winky, who had no genitals and a coat hanger sticking out of his head, was a queer?

Tinky Winky not only has no sex, he doesn't even exist. HE'S A FICTIONAL CHARACTER! So how does anybody come to the conclusion that Tinky Winky is gay? Granted, Tinky is purple, which is a color of gay pride—but it's also the color of grapes. And Tinky has a triangle on his head, which is the symbol of gay pride—but it's also a musical instrument. Maybe Tinky just gets better reception that way.

Either way, this is *Homophobus extremus*, someone so afraid of gays that he goes off the deep end.

It's this kind of lunacy, spoken through the mouth of an ordained (by whom, I would like to know) minister, that keeps the embers of antigay sentiment burning. The match is hatred, and the kindling is crafted from ignorance. It's as simple as that.

Last, but certainly not least, is Pat Robertson. He brings the gravitas of Billy Graham and combines it with the corn-pone qualities of Jim Bakker. The combination is devastating because he almost sounds as if he knows what he is talking about. He draws you in and then smacks you senseless with a sucker punch of self-confident idiocy.

I don't remember how old I was when I first saw him, but I know that seeing him is the reason that I eventually developed eczema. I say this because my dermatologist couldn't tell me what had caused it. Like others of his ilk, Robertson has put together an empire based on a business formula fueled by religious fervor. Like Messrs. Roberts and Falwell, he not only started his own university but also created the Christian Broadcasting Network. Unlike those ministers, however, he skipped the whole church phase and went straight to broadcasting. The airwaves were, and still remain, his chapel.

But the pulpit is not his only outlet for public speaking. In 1988, Robertson ran for president, losing in the primaries—the Republican primaries, I might add.

Today, Robertson appears on his own TV show, *The 700 Club*, where he dishes up a healthy combo of Christianity and the news. His delivery reminds me, disconcertingly, of David Brinkley—if Brinkley was electroshocked into being a born-again Christian. Much like a fine steak with a side of mountain oysters, the result is indigestion.

And Robertson's version of the news makes Fox Network's interpretation look almost like good old-fashioned, responsible, Woodward-Bernstein journalism. He has said things on the airwaves that have made the airwaves feel bad for being airwaves. If he were—God forbid—the only provider of news, I might pray to be deaf.

But then I would miss some of the most amusingly stupid quotes ever. When the folks of Dover, Pennsylvania, voted out all of the school-board members who had introduced the teaching of intelligent design into science classes (as the Christian response to Darwin's godless theory of evolution), here is what Pat told them to expect as a result of such foolhardiness:

"I'd like to say to the good citizens of Dover, if there is a disaster in your area, don't turn to God, you just rejected Him from your city. And don't wonder why He hasn't helped you when problems begin.... Just remember, you just voted God out of your city."

To later underscore this decidedly psychotic point, he would write, "God is tolerant and loving, but we can't keep sticking our finger in His eye forever. If they have future problems in Dover, I recommend they call on Charles Darwin. Maybe he can help them."

My jaw dropped when I read this. My eyes glazed over and I lost the use of my vocal cords. If you really need me to comment on this, then you shouldn't be reading this book. Well, what if God *is* Charles Darwin? Where does that leave Pat?

Finally, the crème de la crème of quotes from the man who once suggested that we nuke our very own State Department. Not to be outdone by his crony, Reverend Falwell, Pat proved he could vent his own prejudice-filled spleen with the best of them.

You better sit down for this one.

The esteemed Pat Robertson once called feminism a "socialist, anti-family political movement that encourages women to leave their husbands, kill their children, practice witchcraft, destroy capitalism, and become lesbians."

I guess it was his Christian sense of charity that prevented him from just calling them the C-word.

As a few of these televangelists have passed from the scene, others have risen to take their place, as if there is some sort of minor league where they hone their skills before they are brought up to the "show." And their legacy is strong. With twenty-four-hour Christian television and radio networks and megachurches that can seat two to three thousand worshippers, it's clear that as long as there is human desperation and despair, there will be a place for the evangelist.

It's a marriage made in heaven.

jesus on a tortilla

One of my favorite news articles of all time appeared in *Newsweek* in 1978. I even made it a part of my stand-up comedy routine for a number of years because, as I always say, the shit you can't make up is always the funniest stuff out there. So, in the long tradition of in-depth investigative reporting, *Newsweek* devoted precious editorial space to chronicle the discovery in New Mexico of an image of Jesus Christ on a tortilla.

And just in case there was some doubt about what you were about to read, the article was actually titled "Jesus on a Tortilla." Now, there's honest journalism. Anyway, Maria Rubio, while preparing a tortilla for her husband, had noticed that the skillet burns resembled Jesus Christ crowned in a wreath of thorns.

That's something that doesn't happen every day. At least, that's how more than 8,000 pilgrims who flocked to her house in Lake Arthur, New Mexico, saw it. That's right, 8,000 pilgrims. Impressive.

I remember reading the piece and wondering what people think they'll gain by visiting the visage of Jesus on a staple of Mexican cuisine. I think I'd just get hungrier, but maybe that's just me. But for hordes of pilgrims, Jesus in any form is a draw. Even in a small town in New Mexico. Even if he's not really there. Even if you could burn a million tortillas and come up with all sorts of images, from Daffy Duck to the Virgin Mary to your second cousin Lenny.

And remember, your distant relatives notwithstanding, there's a long list of locations where Jesus and the Virgin Mary have made appearances. They have shown up in every conceivable type of spot. A crying wall here. A bleeding painting there. A face outlined on a dishrag in Turin. Think of a place, they've made their presence felt.

But how do believers know it's them? No one really knows what either Jesus or his mother, Mary, looked like. What makes pilgrims sure that they're seeing what they think they're seeing? The images we have in our minds of these two merely resemble the pictorial renditions of Jesus and Mary preserved from the Middle Ages.

I realize faith can lead people in any number of directions, but I wonder in this case if it should be to the museum.

When you think about it, these images have been seen—hand on the Bible here—on a pancake, a cinnamon bun, and a grilled-cheese sandwich. And the Jesus image on the last, incidentally, fetched its owner 28,000 bucks. He may have gone hungry for a night, but it's easier to go to bed with your stomach growling when you know you're waking up to the biggest breakfast Denny's serves.

There have also been sightings of Jesus on a cookie sheet, a pizza pan, inside the freezer at a local grocery, on a tree stump, and even on the shell of a turtle. And wherever these images show up, there is always someone there to believe. Somebody whose abiding faith is unshakably reinforced. In this world where technology is exploding, where we are inundated by one man-made image after the next, there's something sweet about the simplicity of a Jesus-on-a-whatever.

Imagine if the Catholic Church, once the Holy See was established in Rome, had decided to turn the images of Jesus and the Virgin Mary into commercial logos. The Catholics could have controlled the world's economy—especially if the pope had blessed every product in the Jesus and Mary line personally. It would have made a corporation like Microsoft look like a mom-and-pop operation.

And the licensing possibilities are endless.

The Jesus and Mary clothing line—"For Fashion Disciples Everywhere!"

Jesus and Mary beauty products—"We Make You Look Simply Divine!"

Jesus and Mary bottled water—"Now in Two Flavors, Holy and Baptismal!"

It would have been so easy, like shooting loaves and fishes

in a barrel. Which is why you have to admire the Church—never a repository of self-restraint—for not making the move into mass marketing. Still, after the past few years of legal attacks against the institution for the indiscretions of the perverts in the priesthood and what it has cost them financially, maybe I should give them a call. Timing is everything.

an ode to *on the road*

When I began writing this book, I had no idea that the fiftieth anniversary of the publication of *On the Road* was in 2007. If we are, indeed, born under stars that guide us, then I would have to consider Jack Kerouac's extraordinary fictional odyssey one of those stars that helped me chart my path.

As I write, I am crisscrossing our splendid country much as Kerouac recounted in his 1957 masterwork. He certainly got it right. There is something wondrous about barrel-assing through the country, eating up the miles as the landscape morphs by.

And no one turned the sense of the excitement that comes from travel and discovery into the expansion of consciousness better than Jack Kerouac. When I read his book for the first time, I got the message loud and clear: Get off your ass and go out into the world and see it for yourself.

As I sit at the window of my tour bus, I see a country filled with people scattered hither and yon—from the never-ending plains of Wyoming, where the nearest neighbor may be miles away, to the clogged highways of Atlanta, where your neighbor may be in the apartment over your head. No matter where these people live, each provides a little thread that is part of the expansive tapestry that is this country.

Each and every one of us has our own way of relating to the universe. We beseech or hosanna or meditate. Some of us feel nature is the governing principle. Some of us feel there is no governing principle.

It is what makes this country rich. It is also what undermines America. In a land that should take great joy in the differences of its people—and in the knowledge that those differences are what make us strong—we generally choose to fear diversity while wallowing in our own stupidity. For a country where so many believe in some sort of God, we seem, as a whole, to have more faith in our ignorance. We seem to find a shared comfort in our fear of those who don't share our beliefs.

I don't know about you, but there just comes a point when I get sick of thinking about religion. It starts to make me crazy. Considering the history of this world, I don't think I can be the only one.

a letter from god's messenger

The high school I went to invited me back during the summer of 2007 to do a benefit performance to raise funds so that it could continue to do what it's been doing since the days when I majored in masturbation. (A double major, actually, as I was ambidextrous.) I leapt at the opportunity to perform my act—stand-up, not the other kind—in the same building I once attended and in support of the school that was partially responsible for making me the man I am today. I say partially because why should they take all of the blame? Oh, there were many more factors, but I haven't the time right now.

Anyway, I relished the idea of taking the stage and finally being able to yell "Fuck!" at the top of my lungs without fear of spending a couple of afternoons in detention. Sophomoric, I know, but we are talking high school here.

And, I must say, it was also nice to be in the position to raise money for an educational institution that had given so much to me and now was in need of the funds to do the same for others. I believe there is nothing more important than education: From it flows everything else. I feel it's more important than religion and, as it teaches you the art of critical thinking, it can, under certain circumstances, even lead you to religion. Religion, on the other hand, might lead you to education, but that usually only happens if you've been jailed and find Jesus and then Jesus says, "Hey stupid, get your GED, I can't understand you when you pray to me."

Now, it's utterly astonishing to me that, in this day and age, you would actually have to raise money for a public high school. What the fuck is the matter with us? When I was a kid they couldn't pump enough money into our education. How do you forget that children—and this is no fucking cliché (well, actually it is, and for good reason)—are our most precious gift and most important resource?

I know this and I don't even have any children, because the state won't allow it. And quite frankly, who can blame them?

There are idiots who bitch about paying property taxes because it goes to education and they don't have any children so why should they have to pay for somebody else's kid's education? Where does thinking like that come from? I have no fucking idea, but I bet they probably go to church. (Okay, that's just conjecture.) I guess those people would prefer to spend public funds to build more prisons to house the tragically uneducated thugs who are going to overrun their communities in the near future.

But I digress. Back to high school. The night that I was giving a little something back, as they say, I also received a little something. I was handed an extraordinary letter from a former classmate. We were not close in high school, though we did know each other, as our class had been together for six years. I was surprised when she handed me the letter, along with a book titled *I Don't Have Enough Faith to Be an Atheist.*

In the letter she said that I was her children's favorite comedian and that her kids ranged in age from seventeen to twenty-eight. She also allowed as how I was very talented, though she felt I shouldn't use the word "fuck" so much. Or, for that matter, at all.

As I have said before, I don't know what word you substitute for *that* word. Nothing has the same punch, the same heart, the same soul, or expresses the same rage as "fuck." See what I mean?

I probably should have stopped reading her letter right there. Or when in the next line she said she didn't enjoy the fact that I made fun of religion and God. At that point I should have known it wasn't going to end well and I should just get on with my life. But as I was writing this book, I thought that reading the letter in its entirety might lead to a revelation or two I could use here. Oh yeah, she was clearly God's messenger—and, by God, I was going to listen.

It turns out that after visiting a Christian bookstore with her seventeen-year-old son, he asked to stop at a traditional bookstore. He saw my book, wanted it, and she bought it for him. To her credit, she then read the book to see if it was appropriate reading for her son. She read my warning directed to those people who generally find their reading at a Christian bookstore. The one where I encourage them to drop the book and back away—far, far away—from it.

Still, she soldiered on, and found what I had written to be extremely offensive. Which is exactly why I wrote the warning in the first place. I seriously didn't want people who obviously weren't going to enjoy the book to read it. It's the same kind of warning pharmaceutical companies put on drugs they sell: "If you experience erections for more than four and a half hours, don't take Viagra."

What else could I do? Lace the cover with chicken blood and have it explode into talcum powder if the person handling the book was wearing a crucifix?

Well, she certainly stuck her nose in the middle of a world that she had, for good reason, avoided until then. In addition to the warning, I also go on to say in the book that "maybe God guided you to this book. . . ." I'll admit it. I wrote that line in hopes of suckering in a few folks who might be looking to take a leap into a different world.

As it turns out, she truly did feel that God had guided her to the book. I mean, it wasn't as if she was looking for it. She didn't even know I had written one. Neither did her son. It saddened her that, as I put it, I didn't have "the required faith to be on the team."

Well, since reading the book, she has been praying for me in the hope that I would develop a personal relationship with God. Which is extremely sweet of her—and I seriously mean that—as she owes me nothing. And I certainly didn't set out to worry all people like her in the world. It's not why I wrote that book.

Then she quotes from a book that has sold a gazillion copies more than mine, *The Purpose-Driven Life*, by Rick Warren. "While life on earth offers many choices, eternity offers only two: heaven or hell. Your relationship to God on earth will determine your relationship to him in eternity."

She then said she doesn't know what my relationship with God is like, but that we will meet in heaven when our time on earth is over. And I should know that God loves me very much.

WHEEEEEEEEEEEEEW!

Okay, there is that part of me that finds this all completely insane, while another part of me—the one my parents taught to respect the beliefs of others—tells me to just smile, shut up, and move on. But you know I can't.

I now have a complete understanding of the Robert Frost poem, the one where he is walking in a yellow wood where two paths diverge and he has to choose one, but he'll always wonder about the other path, the proverbial one not chosen. My classmate and I were roughly the same age and had been born in the same suburb and attended the same high school. But she chose the path that apparently has been snowplowed by Jesus, and I headed up the one where I'm slogging though snowdrifts and slipping and sliding because I am wearing shoes that have no traction.

So she feels I have chosen the wrong path. Well, I feel there's a bit of hubris to that. After all, outside of being a criminal, if you are happy with your path, how can it be the wrong one? Even if you don't find yourself skipping with God.

I am sure I appear to many people to be a blasphemer and a godless sinner. And my classmate isn't the first to criticize me for either my potty mouth or my comical attacks on organized religion. But I see it differently. This is what I do. And if there is a true God, as the Christian world sees him—and it is always a *him*, by the way—I think he'd like me to do what I was born to do.

I mean, talk about a purpose-driven life. I definitely have one. I am the guy who makes the devout Christian feel better about him- or herself. I am the guy who they are afraid their children will listen to. I am the guy who says, "YOU'VE GOTTA BE FUCKIN' KIDDING ME!"

I know her heart is in the right place. I am just not sure if her head is. I have never understood the need of people who believe they have to get everyone else to believe the same things they do. In her case, I guess she felt responsible for my eternal welfare because we went to school together and I somehow have wandered down a wrong path. As she sees it, she's only trying to help out the best way she knows. But why?

As much as I find this all quite funny, I also know that it's not funny to her. I'm laughing because she's worried about me, and she's worried about me because I'm laughing. And that's what it all boils down to. A sense of humor.

If I am sure of anything about the God I may or may not believe in, whoever it is, I am certain that he has a sense of humor.

And I know what my job here on earth is: to make people laugh. And maybe to make them think a little, too.

All I can say is, thank God for that.

the one and only jimmy swaggart

No one was more spectacular, more sartorial, more emphatic, more charismatic, more talented, and more full of shit than the marvelous Mr. Jimmy Swaggart. In a world cluttered with televangelists slinging their horseshit across the airwaves, no one's command of the pulpit was more stunning.

Part of the reason may have been genetic. He was a cousin of one of rock and roll's most lunatic performers, Jerry Lee Lewis, who pounded his piano with an unconscious abandon. Jimmy had just enough of Jerry's wild-eyed lunacy to give his sermonizing a bit of swagger.

As soon as I was introduced to his work, his weekly sermons became something I had to watch. And I obviously was not alone. I followed his progress as his flock grew by leaps and bounds and he moved into larger and larger churches. At the height of his fame, his home congregation in Baton Rouge consisted of more than four thousand members, and at least two hundred television stations ran his program.

What was his secret? The guy was sexy. Not George Clooney sexy, but used-car salesman kind of sexy—you know, à la President Clinton. And his line was mesmerizing.

This guy had no trouble using the words and life of Christ to explain anything and everything. Trust me, one could devote a lifetime to the study of his extraordinary use of the illogical to create a logic all his own. I have never seen anyone to whom the words "silver-tongued devil" applied more. If you watched him regularly, it's easy to understand why the shit he was slinging was so addictive.

By far the best example of his rhetorical flourishes was an apology speech he gave after he had been caught on film at a motel with a prostitute. This occurred at the moment his empire had reached its zenith and his church was bringing in millions of dollars A YEAR.

Not wanting to see his cash cow slaughtered on the altar of a public scandal, Swaggart went before both his congregation and the television cameras and asked for forgiveness.

He was magnificent in defeat. With bowed head, he stood before God and everybody else in his magnificent church—a church, by the way, complete with blood-of-Christ carpeting—and addressed the Lord himself. It was during this very trying time that Mr. Swaggart had what can be described only as a theological breakthrough.

"And most of all," Swaggart began, "to my Lord and my Savior, my Redeemer, the One whom I have served and I love and I worship. I bow at His feet [for He] has saved me and washed me and cleansed me. I have sinned against You, my Lord. And I would ask that Your precious blood would wash and cleanse every stain, until it is in the seas of God's forgetfulness, never to be remembered against me anymore."

The saints be praised—how good is the concept of a God who forgets? Swaggart actually wanted to replace the all-knowing and all-seeing God we had all been schooled on with one with just a bit of memory loss.

The man was a visionary. Bucking thousands of years of Judeo-Christian thought, he was bringing us a new concept of God—one who just doesn't remember everything.

Sweet.

Bringing his thinking process to its natural conclusion, what Jimmy was really asking was: What is so wrong with a married clergyman banging a hooker at the Bates Motel if God is going to forget about it? And while that was, indeed, what he was saying, it is, sadly, not what he meant. Obviously, Jimmy didn't realize what he actually said. He probably wasn't even conscious of it because, if he had been cognizant of what he said, he definitely would have started a new church.

He could have called it the Church of the Forgetting God, where the Lord can only remember a few commandments each week. "This week you only have to be mindful of the First, Second, and Seventh Commandments, and next week only the Fifth Commandment need be obeyed." The artwork over the altar could have been of a God who sits around in a big country club in the sky, sipping martinis. In my mind, I see him with a puzzled look in his eyes that signals he isn't quite grasping all that is going on around him, but with enough of a smile that assures the faithful he is enjoying it a whole lot more.

For someone as crafty as Jimmy Swaggart, I am surprised he didn't push this concept more. In fact, given my theatrical background, I am surprised that *I* haven't.

I was first introduced to the Reverend Swaggart in 1981 while working with my friends Mark Linn-Baker, Paul Schierhorn, and Bill Peters on a show for Joseph Papp's Public Theater in New York City. I will tell you how it all happened in a minute, so please be patient.

In the meantime, Joe Papp had approached Mark (you may remember him as Cousin Larry from television's *Perfect Strangers*) and asked him to do a show at the Public. Mark agreed, on the condition that he could do a show with me.

Mark and I had worked together before at Yale. In those other outings, Mark would do a few of his own set pieces, I would do stand-up comedy, and then we would do some improvisations together. In our early days, it was a way for us to make a little money to get by. To do our laundry, so to speak. Which is the reason we eventually called our show *The Laundry Hour.*

Anyway, Mr. Papp didn't know me, so I was asked to

audition for him. Just me, doing stand-up for Joseph Papp, one of the most innovative producers of the American theater. Just me and the man who had produced *Hair* and *A Chorus Line* and Shakespeare in the Park. Just him, being a legend, and me doing twenty minutes. Just great. Piece of cake.

Let me tell you, there's nothing weirder than performing for one person. And it doesn't get any stranger than performing for one of the great minds of the American theater. It was incredibly nerve-wracking. It also didn't help that I was desperate, both for work and for any form of income. And in case you were wondering, desperation is never a strong basis for performance. But somehow I muddled through it, and Mr. Papp was kind enough to let me work with Mark on the show.

His permission, however, brought us to our next hurdle. What show? We didn't have a show. We had to come up with one from scratch. So we invited Bill to direct the nonexistent show and Paul to write music for it.

After a few discussions, we seemed to settle on some nebulous idea about a show with a religious theme. It was at that point that Paul Schierhorn brought in a cassette recording from a new televangelist by the name of Jimmy Swaggart.

All we had was his voice, but that was enough. It was from the end of his show and we had to rely on Paul to describe the setting. Paul told us Swaggart was sitting on the ground and leaning against a gravestone in the shade of a weeping willow tree. That's when we heard Jimmy say something along the lines of "I am sitting here on my mother's grave, asking you to send me money so that I can continue to spread the word of the Gospel. I am here because I know that she would want you to do that."

You just had to love a guy who had the big brass nuts to invoke his dead mother as a reason for us to send in our hard-earned cash. I was impressed. The only thing that would have been better was if he had said that she was still alive and that he would dig her up only if we started making our cash pledges *now.*

We listened in awe. And that was the moment that our play first began to take real shape. Mark and I would be evangelists. Only our church would be a Church of Comedy. Instinctively we saw the similarities between religion and comedy—and Jimmy Swaggart gave us an idea, and the inspiration to write it. It was his complete shamelessness about shilling and bullshitting that gave us the basis for our characters and our church.

When the curtain went up that first night, we were dressed in choir robes with big bow ties.

I know it is strange to go into a play at this point, but it is truly the best way to conclude this book. Or maybe it isn't. I really don't know. I do know, however, it's as clear as I can be about my feelings about what I do and what I believe in.

To be honest, when the play was done, the audiences—though small—loved it. No one really knew us (*Perfect*

Strangers was still a few years in the future) so, I think, our show was something of a pleasant surprise. Also, *The Laundry Hour* was short, which is always a crowd-pleaser.

Joe Papp told us to just keep running the show, that we would build an audience, and not to worry about what the critics had to say. All of our friends, in the meantime, said the critics would love it.

Since we were all a little desperate to be noticed, we did let the show run. So in came the critics. And they hated it. I still have to wonder who could hate something that short. We never gave anyone enough time to work up a hate.

In retrospect, however, there is one thing I do know for sure. *The Laundry Hour* was way ahead of its time.

The year is 1981. The president is Ronald Reagan.

And now, the curtain rises on . . .

the laundry hour

a play by
Mark Linn-Baker,
Lewis Black,
and William Peters
with music and lyrics
by Paul Schierhorn

VOICE: And now, Ladies and Gentlemen, the Public Theater proudly presents—Mark Linn-Baker and Lewis Black, starring in *The Laundry Hour.*

(RELIGIOUS PLAY ON; MARK AND LEW ENTER IN FLOWING ROBES)

LEW: Thank you, Cantor Schierhorn, for that beautiful and instructive opening.

MARK: Good evening, everyone. I'm Mark.

LEW: I'm Lew.

MARK: I'm a comic.

LEW: I'm a Jew. As you may have gathered from our vestments, Mark and I have prepared a very special evening for you.

MARK: It's true. Lew and I have struggled as comics for years now, but it's only recently that we saw the light and were born again into comedy. Just in the nick of time.

LEW: Hallelujah, Brother Mark!

MARK: Praise the Lord.

LEW: Brothers and Sisters, Mark and I are filled with the spirit of satire this evening.

MARK: I feel it.

LEW: We are pleased as punch to be here with all of you dear people here at the Public Theater. You know, this old building is going to rock tonight! Look at those lovely, expectant faces out there.

MARK: Oh, my heart is full. I have to share this with you, Brother Lew.

LEW: What's that, Mark?

MARK: I think this is an enlightened audience.

LEW: Yes, you really are.

MARK: Hallelujah.

LEW: Praise God.

MARK: God be praised!

LEW: Blessed be the name of the Lord.

MARK: Hosanna!

LEW: Lordy, Lordy!

MARK AND LEW: EYAHOO!!! AMEN!

LEW: You got it, Brothers and Sisters, welcome to an evening of comedy and religion. Just in the nick of time.

MARK: You know the roots of comedy and the roots of religion all stem from the same source. And what is that source?

LEW: Death! That's right, comedy and religion is our sniveling way of coming to grips with the big one. You know, as the ancient Jews once said, "Yisgadal v'yiskadash, sh'mei rabbah."

MARK: Now, later on this evening we're going to give you a religious experience that many of you will never forget, and that's when Lew will give himself over entirely to the power of the holy joke, in the healing portion of our show.

You know, friends, until Lew and I were born again into comedy, we had a pretty rough time dealing with social issues in our act. We were looking for a way to combine humor and social elements, and—well, we made a lot of mistakes along the way. We were just starting out in the business. Back then, we would have started our show something like this.

(BLACKOUT; SNAPPY PLAY ON; LIGHT UP ON MARK AND LEW IN LOUD JACKETS)

VOICE: Ladies and Gentlemen, the Public Theater proudly presents Mark Linn-Baker and Lewis Black in *The Laundry Hour*!

MARK:

(BRANDISHING NEWSPAPER)

HEYYY! Thank you, thank you, thank you. Good evening. I'm Mark.

LEW: I'm Lew.

MARK: I'm a comic.

LEW: Me too!

MARK: I see here that the ERA is having a lot of trouble being passed.

LEW: Boy, that really pisses me off. I was in a bar the other night...

MARK: Yeah?

LEW: Yeah, and a woman came in—you're gonna love this story—a woman came in and went up to the bartender.

MARK: Right?

LEW: Mmmmhmmm. And she's got a duck under her arm. Bartender says, "We don't serve *pigs* here!"

MARK: Yeah?

LEW: Right—and the lady says, "This ain't a pig, it's a duck!"

MARK: Yeah? Yeah?

LEW: The bartender says, "I was talking to the duck, lady!"

(RIM SHOT)

Thank yewww!

MARK:

(LOOKING AT NEWSPAPER)

Oh! I see the Poles are in the news again.

LEW: They're a fabulous group of people. They're in trouble, too—but can anyone here tell me the difference between a Polish woman and a bowling ball?

(PAUSE)

That's right, you can *eat* the bowling ball!

(RIM SHOT)

Thank yewww! And speaking of bowling balls, you know, the Pope is hung like a horse, and one day he gets out of the shower . . .

(BLACKOUT; RELIGIOUS MUSIC PLAYS; LIGHTS UP ON MARK AND LEW IN ROBES, WATCHING MONITOR AND CHUCKLING)

MARK: Whew. We were pretty raw.

LEW: Yes, we were. We got away with murder.

MARK: It would be a different story tonight, wouldn't it?

LEW: Yeah. Lots of moxie, but not insights. No *truth* to the material.

MARK: So we changed. As you all know, Lew and I and Paul received MFAs in entertainment. We became pros. We got our Equity cards.

(THEY REVEAL THEIR EQUITY CARDS, WHICH ARE ON CHAINS AROUND THEIR NECKS)

We simplified our style. Put in a touch of class. Watch.

(THEY LOOK AT THE MONITOR; BLACKOUT; "LAUNDRY HOUR VAMP"; MARK AND LEW ENTER WEARING STRAW HATS AND HOLDING NEWSPAPERS)

MARK: Hey, Lew.

LEW: Hey, Mark. I was in Central Park the other night.

MARK: No kidding!

LEW: This mugger comes up to me and says, "Give me all your money."

MARK: What'd you do?

LEW: I gave him all my money.

MARK AND LEW:

We're the Laundry Hour
We are the show
We've got laffs for you
'Cause we're in the know
And we love you love you love you
We love you love you love you love you love
That's the way it goes
We never close
We're the Laundry Hour

MARK: Hey, Lew.

LEW: Hey, Mark.

MARK: A woman went into a bar the other day with a duck under her arm.

LEW: No kidding.

MARK: She asked the bartender for a drink.

LEW: What happened?

MARK: The damn pig insulted her!

MARK AND LEW:

We're the Laundry Hour
We are the boys
Beat your palms together now and then
'Cause we like the noise
Plus we love you, love you love you,
We love you love you love you love you love...

(BLACKOUT; RELIGIOUS MUSIC; LIGHTS UP ON MARK AND LEW)

MARK: Wow! Did we goof on that one!

LEW: God doesn't like glitz.

MARK: We were so intent on telling the truth, we forgot the jokes! Finally we worked things out. I should say, He worked things out for us.

What I think we need, what I think we can look forward to these next few years, is a return to Fundamentalist

Comedy. What I'm asking for—what I'm hoping for—is that we'll be able to get back to those beliefs and those values that made this great country of ours funny. It's interesting—we now have a president—a president with a show business background and a president with a sense of humor. Here's a man who was shot, and on the way to the hospital, on the way to the operating room—this man let loose with a flurry of jokes. As they're putting him under with anesthesia, here's a man who looks up from the table, staring death in the face, and he says to his doctors, "Tell me you're Republicans." Now, that's a funny line. And under the circumstances it took great courage and timing.

The pope, now—we've got a pope—he's a great performer. He's got a sense of humor. Now, this guy gets shot, and as they're putting him out at the hospital, he looks up at the doctors—he could have gone for a cheap line—he looks up at the doctors and says, "Tell me you're Republicans." Now, these are funny men. And I should point out, it's very hard to kill these guys. Something to think about.

LEW: Right now, Mark and Paul and I are going to get down on our hands and knees and pray for you.

Dear God. Mark and I and Paul are just a little sick and tired of banging our heads against the brick wall you call, ha, opportunity. We're bloodied and bowed, but not daunted because we know as we smack our heads against that door and our brains spill on the floor here, that you'll pick them up and do something with them, something else, I hope. It's not been good for us, Lord. Our mission is not an easy one. Mark actually did his first tax form this year, and I'm just a little sick and tired of being a write-off. We have habits, Lord, we can't help it. We're just anonymous little creatures—tiny pieces of undiscovered comic excrement swirling around on the big planet Earth, searching for just a STINKING POSTAGE STAMP OF ENOUGH STUFF. I'M TALKING ABOUT SOMETHING ON THE STAMP.

(MARK CALMS HIM DOWN)

Please, Dear Lord, move us from the Public Theater into a larger space, a much larger space. Big. Where there are usherettes. Hundreds of them. Wearing pasties, and who say things like, "Lew, how's tricks?" In the name of the Father and the Son and . . . Marilyn Monroe, may she rest in peace, because boy would I love a piece of her. Bring her over to the house, Lord, dead or alive, I don't care . . .

(MARK CALMS HIM DOWN)

Amen.

And now, Brother Mark will sing for you.

(LEW EXITS)

MARK: Hey, okay, this is the barnyard song. Can we have some houselights, please? I want you all to join in as we go along. You should be able to figure it out pretty quickly. Just join in as you feel it. As we do the chicken verse. Ready? Okay, here we go...

barnyard song

MARK (INTROS SONG)

CHICKEN VERSE (MARK CLUCKS LIKE A CHICKEN, ASKS THE AUDIENCE TO JOIN IN)

Hey, okay. We got a few people to join in there. And God bless you. God bless you for that. You know, when I think of chickens, I cannot help but think, I'm ashamed to say, of this great country of ours in the last few years. We feathered our nest and were content to sit with our heads under our wings. But the fox has slipped back into the old henhouse. Well, maybe it's time we woke up and found that chicken in our hearts. Wring him by his neck until his little beady eyes pop out! Maybe it's time we found courage to restore the eagle that once reigned there. Yes, maybe we'll find that courage as we sing this next verse. The pig verse. Ready? Ho-Ho.

PIG VERSE (MARK OINKS)

Okay! Got a few more people to join in that time. And God bless ya. I think we're gonna get everyone singing before this song is over. Ho-ho! You know, I remember it wasn't too long ago that I was out on the street yelling, "Pig, Pig, Pig." And I wasn't calling the herd. Those times are gone. The day that chicken walked into my heart. I crossed that street. I got to the other side. I bowed my head and started walking along with everyone else. Kind of like a sheep. And that brings us to the next verse. The sheep verse. Here we go. Join in as you feel it.

SHEEP VERSE (MARK BAAHS)

Hey. Okay. Yeah. Yeah. I think we had—maybe not everyone singing on that one but—quite a number of people—and God bless you. God bless you—and God bless this great country of ours. Yeah—you know all those sheep marching along together, heads bowed. I remember, I remember black sheep. The black sheep were marching along with the white sheep. But now it seems they're cutting those black sheep out and herding them into some other corral. Civil Rights! There's a couple of words you haven't heard in a while. Woo hoo. They're gone—gone. They're called Human Rights now. Any minorities here tonight? Just raise your hands. You know who you are. Good luck to you! Good luck to you in the years to come.

Well, maybe it's better to have a sacrificial lamb or two than to slaughter a sacred cow. Hey, and that leads us to the next verse, the cow verse. Okay, ladies only on this one. Let's go!

COW VERSE (MARK MOOS)

Heyyy, I think we lost a few heifers on that one! You know, a lot of very powerful people are starting to think the ERA is about as useful as tits on a bull. But things aren't so bad—I see there's a woman sitting on the Supreme Court. Well, maybe that's a fair trade for losing the right to abortion. After all, we can't be fighting like cats and dogs all the time—and that brings us to the dog verse—everybody, let's go!

DOG VERSE (MARK BARKS)

Now, I want everyone to join in this last verse. I want everyone to pick their favorite animal. Pick any animal you want. Because you still have the freedom to do that—for the moment. Okay, pick that animal and I want to hear the whole barnyard singing and carousing together, like one happy farm—OKAY!

BARNYARD VERSE (MARK MAKES A VARIETY OF BARNYARD SOUNDS)

(MARK EXITS AS LEW ENTERS)

LEW: Thank you, Mark, for that stirring and uplifting spiritual. It's on our album—*Songs of Animal Resistance*—which we'll be selling in the lobby after the show. You know, I'm feeling great tonight, and I hope you are too, because I felt the power of the laugh in this room, and we need that precious laughter in these terrible and troubled times in which we live.

As Mark's song pointed out—as we swing into the eighties, it gets tougher and tougher, for animals and humans alike, to stand up and laugh at what they believe in. A wise man once said, "The truth shall make you free." An even wiser man replied, "The truth hurts." And I'm here to tell you tonight that these past few years, the Truth has been a pain in the ass!

The only way to live with the Truth these days is to laugh at it. And what is the Truth? Well, the Truth is there is some guilt lying about here, Brothers and Sisters. I can feel it. The guilt of being indoors for the past ten years while some of the things you cared so much about died in the streets. But let's face it, it got a little dangerous out there. You won the battle to give the streets back to the people, and as a result, you stay locked in your apartment. You're surrounded by issues that are busting your balls and ball-ettes, and there don't seem to be easy answers anymore.

Now, you probably came here this evening with a little trepidation in your hearts. You probably came here tonight thinking that this offering of ours would be some kind of political *J'accuse*, hmnn? You worried that we would shriek at you, "Shame, shame" for trying to make a lot of money. For using that small nest egg to play the market. Not tonight, Brothers and Sisters, not tonight because we want you to be free of guilt and full of laughter. Goddammit, go out there. Make it hand over fist, any way you can! If you've got to screw somebody—screw them to the wall! So your building is going co-op. Fine. Make that deal and kick out the four black families and the elderly white folk, and turn that old building into a nice piece of real estate. Rake it in! Invest in uranium, silver, and chrome in Rhodesia. It's your pearl, so you suck on it. Suck it dry. We all deserve a piece of the pie. Or a pizza pie. Canned food will do! And be free of guilt? Is that what you're telling me, Brother Lew? Yes, because that's where we come in. Mark and I will give you the healing power of social satire. You can rest secure in the thought that Mark and I are hard at work, laughing all your troubles away.

(PAUSE)

I know what you're thinking—where do we get the guts and the faith to go on, huh? It's hard. It gets harder each year. I'll be honest with you, we need cash. Cold hard cash. Gold fillings, a bauble or two, anything, so we can pursue the work of banishing guilt and trauma and even sexual frustration from this great land of ours. Your money will go directly, and I mean directly, into cleaning up the stinking rattrap of an apartment that Mark and I live in. Right now we're spending too much of our precious time laughing away the filth we live in instead of laughing for you. A couch! All we need is a couch that comes free of lice. A chair with four legs. A cat for our litter box.

We have plans for a crusade across the whole planet.

(TAKING OUT PHOTOS)

I'm talking about franchises of mini-churches. Exact replicas of Our Smiling Church of Christ and the Holy Joke (sauna included) that we're building in Tucson, Arizona. This is where we will be housing our church's prize collection of relics.

(HOLDS UP A BONE)

. . . Will Rogers' funny bone.

(HOLDS UP A JAR)

Mort Sahl's tongue . . .

(HOLDING UP A JAR)

. . . and Lenny Bruce's middle finger.
And you can purchase replicas of these relics tonight along with that LP I mentioned earlier.

And miracles. You want miracles? This man—

(WHEELS OUT GURNEY)

—died last night while brooding over the president's fiscal policies. He's cold as last week's mashed potatoes—

(HE TAPS THE BODY'S LEG WITH A HAMMER)

—but I will personally resurrect him with a joke, in the lobby after the show. He's yours for $6.98. A great little gift for the kids.

And we need the buckos, Brothers and Sisters. Right now this is but a dream. Money is tight these days, and with the current budget, you have to have a bullet for a head to get so much as a dime. Well, we're no crybabies. And I'm going to tell you a secret, because you folks have been the most wonderful audience we've ever played to. We have been talking to people so powerful I can't even mention their names, and we are going to be the first church to get its own MX missile. Why an MX? Because it's supposed to be hidden, right? Well, what better place to hide it than with the two of us. Hell, our agent doesn't even know where we are half the time. Now, I know missiles aren't funny, but they help pay the rent. And if a country stops laughing, we'll blow them back to the Stone Age. Our country knows what funny is. Reagan tries. He even goes out and gets shot for a laugh. Then we get General Haig with his eyes popping out yelling, "I'm in charge here, I'm in charge." That's funny! And we're funny too—every night except Monday—unless they kick us out, because there are people out there who fear the Laugh of God! They're scared of the Smiling Christ. It makes me want to puke. But we won't go. Not without a fight.

And if they take us away, our home phone number is in the program.

(HE HAS PULLED A GUN AND IS RAVING; MARK ENTERS;)
(MARK TAKES THE GUN AND LEAVES)

I would like to introduce our special guest this evening. Although Mark and I trained in comedy, neither of us had any religious training. We met this man when he was on his first American tour—in a mall in Passaic, New Jersey. Please join me in a generous welcome to the Maharishi Baba Yoga.

MAHARISHI BABA YOGA: I would like to talk to you this evening about spiritual growth. The growth of the spirit. Oftentimes, in our lives, we feel a longing for something more. We feel that there must be more to this life. And truly, it is written, "In the beginning was the Word." And the Word was "More." We all had to become One with the Word. To join in the oneness of the Word. To embrace the One. Anyone. (LOOKS INTO AUDIENCE) Maybe that one. Now. How do we go about embracing the One? We learn how to embrace the One through the four Truths. The first Truth is that there is suffering. I suffer, you suffer—let's face it, we're unhappy. The second Truth is that you are the cause of your own suffering. The third Truth is that you can rid yourself of the suffering. And the fourth Truth is that you rid yourself of the suffering by following the path. What is the path? You find this path through a teacher. This teacher must be one who embraces the One. Now. At any given moment there is only one person on the face of the Earth who is the embodiment of the embracing of the One. And lucky for you. That is me. We are all clouded by the world of Samsara—the world of illusion. We are all lost in this world. Our minds are clouded by this illusory thought. Let me give a simple demonstration of the clouding of the mind by Samsara.

(ASKS FOR VOLUNTEER)

Would you think of a number from one to ten? Are you thinking of that number? Is that number four? Yes? Thank you. You see, because I embrace the One I am able to know the oneness of the world, to see the oneness, to know a simple number in the mind of another.

(ASKS ANOTHER VOLUNTEER)

Is that number six? No? You see, your mind is clouded with Samsara. With illusory thought. If your mind had not been clouded, we would have had the same number. Now. Let us move on to the meditation. To the teaching. I would like if we would all join, for a few moments, in a brief experience of the embracing of the One. Now. Everyone, please—sit straight. Your back is straight. Both of your feet are on the floor. The head rests on the shoulders. Now, close your eyes. You—you, sir. You are tilted to one side. You seem to be—I see your wallet is in your pocket. Just take your wallet out of your pocket. Just set it down. Now close your eyes. Let your mind become nothing. Let your mind become empty. Let the thoughts as they occur float away like little balloons floating off into the air—they disappear. They are gone. The mind becomes empty. You see the mind is like a mirror. If it is stained, you stain the reflection of the world, but if it is clear, then you reflect the oneness of the world. All right. Thank you. Open your eyes. Now, was there one of you who perhaps very strongly felt the One. Felt at one with the world. Felt the embracing of the One. Is there such a one? Yes? You felt it? Now, can I ask you, do you have a steady job? Visa card? MasterCard? No? Is there someone else? Yes? Do you have a steady job? MasterCard, Visa card, a good credit rating? Any mortgages or liens? I see. Very good. It is perhaps time for you to come and live at the Ashram. Do not quit your job, but simply come to think or pursuing your study at the Center. All right. Now. I must leave you this evening but first I would like to tell you a story. Once there was a man who had a teacher. And although he tried very very hard, he could not always do exactly what his teacher asked him to do. One day this man was hit by a truck. And he did not die quickly. Thank you.

LEW: By now, many of you are probably thinking to yourselves, "Comedy and religion—yes—of course—it seems so right!" It's no accident that Mark and I are here tonight. It is all part of God's divine plan, and we'll be offering all of you the chance to take Comedy into your own hearts later this evening. But first I would like to share with you a personal history of my own conversion—the remarkable story of my own rebirth in Comedy. It came to me in a vision one night. It was Election Eve, 1980, and America was about to hitch its wagon to a twenty-mule-team star. Mark was out of commission with a gentleman's complaint and I was doing a solo somewhere in Ohio . . .

(RIPPLE DISSOLVE TO LEW ON NIGHTCLUB STAGE)

lew's club routine

(RIPPLE DISSOLVE UP ON CINCINNATI)

LEW: . . . but not only that, he wants Goebbels as his secretary of state. Thank you. You're a wonderful audience. Always a pleasure to be in Cincinnati. Can you believe those Republicans? They meet up in Detroit, they get rid of the ERA and abortion, and we're lucky they didn't decide to bring back slavery. What do you mean it's a good idea? Jesus Christ! I'll tell you the problem with Reagan is that he's bringing back Kissinger. I can't believe it—in any civilized country in the world he'd have been tried for war crimes. Not here. No. I'm a yid bob. I'm Jewish. So is he. But he's also a Nazi. You can't be a Jew and a Nazi at the same time. It's impossible. Why? Because Jews are born genetically liberal. Kike? What do you mean, kike? What rock did you crawl out from under? Listen, it wasn't my idea to do a phone company convention. My agent called and said it might be nice. "Reach out and touch someone." Well, touch this! I give up!

(LEW THROWS DOWN HIS NEWSPAPER AND HAS A TANTRUM)

You want a joke? I've got a joke for you. There was this Polish woman who walked into a bar with a bowling ball under her arm... you're gonna love this...

(LEW HAS A HEART ATTACK AND DIES)

The first thing I saw was my body on the floor of the club. It was the biggest laugh I had gotten all night. I wanted to stick around but I started to drift upward through a mist. The stage receded further as I moved down what seemed a dimly lit corridor. In the distance I saw a door. It was a blue door. And on it was a sign that said "MEN'S." I pushed it open, and went inside. All I could see was a bunch of clouds. Then I heard people going, "Mr. Black, Mr. Black, Mr. Black..."

(MARK ENTERS)

MARK: Mr. Black!
LEW: Yes? And there was this human being of light.
MARK: That was a tough crowd you were working.
LEW: What's going on?
MARK: Come with me.
LEW: Where am I?
MARK: You're sort of dead, Mr. Black.
LEW: What?
MARK: Please. Our time together is short. I have to show you a few things. Follow me—through these clouds.

(50'S MUSIC)

Look, Mr. Black—it's Election Eve, 1956, and America is about to snuggle under a blanket of cozy prosperity with Ike and Mamie. Do you see that?

LEW: It's my elementary school.

MARK: And inside that school—there—a little curly-headed boy with a hook for a nose . . .

LEW: It's me!

MARK: Look—the teacher is gone and you're up in front of the class, doing your classic fallout shelter routine. You're very funny and the other children are laughing—and look, there in the back—a little blond-haired girl . . .

LEW: Sally McKenzie!

MARK: Yessss, little Sally McKenzie—a Wasp, Lewis—and you *know* what that means! Silky skin and dimpled thighs and just the beginning of downy hair on her forearms—looking at you, laughing at you, pounding her desk with hilarity—and next to her, do you see *him*? Who's that?

LEW: It's Jimmy Whitlock.

MARK: Yes, little Jimmy Whitlock, a lonely boy who is desperately trying for a laugh by making farting noises under his arm. But the class can't take its eyes off you as you start to make fun of President Eisenhower's bald head! Your eyes find Sally McKenzie's and a sudden slight moistness appears around her parted lips . . . Come with me!

LEW: Wait a minute!

MARK: There's more, Lewis! Look. A university campus in the flowering turmoil of 1968. And look, that dark-haired boy with the bullhorn—looks like he's had a nose job—

he's haranguing the crowd with one-liners—and beside him—who is that?

LEW: Hannah Jones.

MARK: Hannah Jones! She's beautiful—a Nubian princess and a fiery radical. You press against each other—activism is like a fever in your blood. Her liquid brown eyes flash approval as the crowd cheers your joke about . . . Lyndon Johnson?

LEW: The one about my wanting to do to Hannah what LBJ'd been doing to the country.

MARK: Yes, yes, that's the one. My God, Lew, that was funny. But look—at the back of the crowd, who is that vacant young man with the long stringy hair?

LEW: It's Jimmy Whitlock.

MARK: Yes. And he's pleased that the strike has shut down the university because he was suspended for hitting the campus security guard in the face with a pie.

LEW: He was never a class act.

MARK: Over here, Mr. Black. Quickly. Look.

LEW: It's a cabaret.

MARK: Time?

LEW: Late at night, Election Day, 1976. The Me Generation has crawled up its own navel and doesn't know what sex it is anymore.

MARK: Very good, Mr. Black. You see her?

LEW: Melissa Champion.

MARK: Yes, Melissa Champion. An intelligent, self-possessed woman of impeccable taste who has an admirable sense of her own individuality. A beacon in the struggle for women's independence . . . with cleavage that just won't quit. Melissa Champion, who has come to see you work the room tonight, Lew, and you were sensational.

LEW: No . . .

MARK: Listen to me! The cabaret is empty except for the two of you, and you murmur your casual witticisms about the welfare system in your offhand way and she is entranced. And the look through the laughter in her eyes is something close to amazement, isn't it? Her self-determining hair brushes against her intellectual shoulders as she stares at your never-ending fount of humor.

LEW: What?

MARK: But look, the door to the kitchen swings open, and a busboy appears, wiping his hands on his grimy apron.

LEW: Oh no.

MARK: Yes.

MARK AND LEW: Jimmy Whitlock.

MARK: Yes, Jimmy Whitlock, and he lives by himself, and the walls of his room are plastered with pictures of his two favorite comedians—Jerry Lewis and Bruno Hauptmann—and he spends his days before a mirror, entertaining an audience of one with a joy buzzer and a bottle of seltzer.

(MARK LEAVES)

Come with me, Mr. Black.

MARK: Over here, Mr. Black. Quickly.

LEW: What a beautiful beach.

MARK: Yes.

LEW: Where are we?

MARK: Aruba.

LEW: I've never been to Aruba.

MARK: I know. (CHECKS WATCH) Okay, let's go. One more vision, then we must send you back

LEW: Send me back?

MARK: Yes. You have important work to do elsewhere . . . and even there you have so little time.

LEW: What do you mean?

MARK: Look, Lewis. Look at your *future*! See that airy sunlit room?

LEW: Yes. And a lot of plants. Lots of vitamins—a shitload of cocaine. And people, sitting around a desk in a hot tub.

MARK: Yes, Lew, L.A.! And that young man is your agent. The older man is a big Hollywood producer. He's seen your act and will suck your cock in order to get the screen rights.

LEW: What?

MARK: Never mind. The door of the office opens.

LEW: Who is that?

MARK: It's Diane, the executive's daughter. Diane Livingstone. She's beautiful isn't she? Blond, tanned, tawny, lithe.

LEW: Shut up!

MARK: And she's walking toward you, isn't she? She's got a copy of your latest album, which will be on sale in the lobby after the show, and it's nestled between her armpit and her left breast. You feel her warmth on it as she presses a script into your hands.

LEW: Shut up.

MARK: And she doesn't say anything, but she looks at you meaningfully for just a second before she turns and swirls out of the office in her summer dress. Her scent is still in the air. In the script, there is a note in feminine handwriting . . . and what is it you read?

LEW: "I didn't know anyone cared so much about people anymore. I laughed until I came. Thank you. Di."

MARK: Now you walk out to your car and drive to the studio gate. There's something familiar about the armed guard at the gate, isn't there. Who is that fellow?

LEW: Oh no, not him again.

MARK: Yes!

MARK AND LEW: Jimmy Whitlock!

MARK: Yes, Jimmy Whitlock, who never made it in the East and moved to California, hoping for a break. And now he works part-time as a security guard at the studio, and he's got a gun permit and a simply enormous heater strapped to his thigh, and he waves you out of the parking lot with a rubber chicken, calling "Congratulations" with a thin smile.

LEW: He wants to kill me!

MARK: Yes . . . and before you know it, Lewis, you will be there.

LEW: Where?

MARK: At the top of your profession—the zenith, the apex, the acme, the Hyperion. And why? Why did you come so far with so little?

LEW: Because I was funny.

MARK: Ah, if only it were that simple. Yes, Lew, you were funny, you are funny, and you will get even funnier, but why are you funny?

LEW: I give up.

MARK: Because you are also meaningful.

LEW: So?

MARK: You are socially relevant. And why are you socially relevant? Why do you always lash out with laughter against the pains and evils of society? Why do you expend the sweat of a lifetime abusing, belittling, castigating, and deriding your betters? What is at the heart of your savage thrusts and parries? One odd circumstance.

LEW: What circumstance?

MARK: You don't get laid.

LEW: What?

MARK: You heard me! You're a celibate, a monk, a priest of comedy. Look, Lew—did you ever wind up making it with Melissa Champion?

LEW: No.

MARK: What about Hannah Jones? Ever get into her pants?

LEW: No.

MARK: What about Sally McKenzie?

LEW: No.

MARK: Well, Jimmy Whitlock did.

LEW: What?!? That's not fair. I'm the funny one!

MARK: Yes, you are, and Jimmy's a jerk, but he's going to make you a legend.

LEW: When?

MARK: In his own time. It's the Lord's will, Lewis. He has chosen a difficult path for you. He has dammed up your seminal fluids, Lewis. He has diverted the river of desire that roars through your loins for a higher purpose. You've been a driven man, Lewis, and now it's even going to be more so. Because you're going to be famous, Lew. Rising out of nothing to a fiery blaze. And Jimmy Whitlock will be there with you, watching all those women, chicks, their damp female faces in those overheated clubs, staring at you adoringly, their mouths parted in laughter, their minds ablaze with social insights so blinding their eyes sparkle. So, you don't get laid. In the end you will be a legend. You'll be onstage one night, in a glow of bastard amber—sleep now, Lew, sleep now, Lew—and you'll hear the walls rock to the sound of laughter. Your thoughts, your insights, your telling observations of contemporary society. Everyone cares what you think. Well, almost everyone, for out of the corner of your eye, you see a blur of movement. Another figure is also rising suddenly from the table and heading for the stage. And he's got a gun in his hand. And the moments are moving very swiftly now, but you just have time to see the flash of a red rubber nose . . .

shooting stars (SUNG BY PAUL SCHIERHORN)

All my life I've thought about shooting stars
Chunks of metal flashing through the night
Shooting stars
Blazing out of darkness
Running toward the light
Come from out of nowhere
They must be going somewhere
Shooting stars

All my life I've had a place hard to find
Stairway to a secret stage in my mind
Everyone must see me before I burn away

It took so long to get here
I'd really like to stay
Shooting stars, shooting stars

Everybody knows him from his photograph
Everybody hears his voice on interviews
Night after night he's on the evening news
Silly boy

Nobody asked you they just put you here
You walk around awhile and then you disappear
I wonder where they'll have you this time next year
Silly boy, silly boy

All my life I've dreamed about shooting stars
Chasing after limousines, dodging cars
I didn't want it to end this way
There was nothing else to do
I watched myself, watch myself
Watch me, watching you
And now that neither you nor I exist
We're born anew
Shooting stars, shooting stars, shooting stars,
Shooting stars, shooting stars

LEW: And that's exactly the way it happened in Cincinnati, that night—seven months ago. Amazing! Extraordinary!

Phenomenal! But don't believe a word of it. Well, the Lord works in mysterious ways. He reached down and picked me up from the floor of that club and I went out and faced 150 people who until that night had devoted their entire lives to the phone company—and I raved at them for two and a half hours and I have no idea what I said to them, but . . . not one of those people works for the phone company anymore. Can you believe it? Thirty-two are Carmelite nuns, laughing away sores in South America. And I have here a letter that is just unbelievable. A woman in Arizona wrote to me and said, "Dear Brother Lew, until the night I saw your act I thought I would be working as a phone company operator for my entire life. After I saw you I quit the phone company—I took correspondence courses and in a few weeks I will be the first female Justice on the Supreme Court!" Can you believe that? I don't know what I did that night—all I know is that the Lord touched me with the Holy Joke, and He touches me with it every night—I can feel it, Brothers and Sisters—I can feel it coming into me right now. Yes, yes, I can feel it.

(MARK ENTERS AND HELPS LEW OFFSTAGE)

Bring me Caspar Weinberger's head!

(LEW EXITS)

MARK: And now, the moment we have all been waiting for this evening. Lew is going to go now—opening his soul to the Laugh of God. But before we bring him back to heal so that we may cleanse our souls, just a word of warning about what you are about to see. The awesome power of social satire can be a wonderful thing, but, please—Dear God—please don't try this at home! In the hands of the professionals this can be a powerful healing tool, but in the hands of the inexperienced it can be dangerous, overly cynical, and downright acerbic. So please leave this to those who can harness this power for good—to us, the professionals. And now, Lew, do you feel it? Do you feel the Laugh of God?

LEW:

(OFFSTAGE)

I feel it!

MARK: Ladies and Gentlemen—so's we can all sleep a little easier tonight, here he is, that high priest of Fundamentalist Comedy—Brother Lewis Black.

(LEW ENTERS)

Heal us! I feel there's someone here tonight—he's possibly a lawyer—he's got—this man is worried about the increasing influence over all our lives of the multinational corporations. What can you do for him, Lew? What can you do for this man, Lew?

(LEW THROWS A PIE IN HIS OWN FACE)

LEW: You're healed now!

MARK: Now, Lew—we have a young man, or a young woman, I don't know which . . .

LEW: Well, get him an operation!

MARK: . . . and a troubled young soul—a casualty of the recent war of sexual liberation.

LEW: Oh, I know that one!

MARK: Yes, Lew? What can you give this person to soothe his aching soul?

(LEW SQUIRTS HIMSELF WITH SELTZER)

MARK: The fear is gone, the pain is gone, the GUILT is gone. Lew, we have a woman, a young woman . . .

LEW: Well, get her number!

MARK: . . . and there's a gentle swell to her belly. She's concerned, as well she might be, about the loss of her right to an abortion. Lew, she needs you. What can you do for her?!?

(LEW PUTS A LAMPSHADE ON HIS HEAD AND BLOWS A HORN)

MARK: We have someone here who feels guilty for moving away from the inner city—for failing to do anything about the sad plight of the inner city. What can you do? What can you say to him?

LEW:

(WITH A RUBBER CHICKEN IN HIS PANTS)

Suck on this! The holy chicken!

LEW AND MARK: Hallelujah! The guilt is gone!

MARK: We'd like to leave you with our final hymn, but first . . . Thanks to our musical director, Paul Schierhorn; our stage manager, Evan Canary; our director, Bill Peters; our business manager, Jimmy Whitlock; our producer, Mr. Joe Papp; and our executive producer . . .

(MARK INDICATES HEAVEN)

hymn (SUNG BY LEWIS AND MARK)

Laugh and the world laughs with you
Cry and you cry alone
Tears are too easy
Sorrow is sleazy
Laughter's your refuge
Your comfort
Your home.

LEW: You know, Brothers and Sisters, you'd have to be goddamned blind not to see the miracles that took place on this stage here tonight. We could have brought out 150 lepers and cured them, but that would have been too easy. On your way out to the lobby this evening, we'll be selling a few things, but this evening we have a real treat for you. You know, there's something to be said for hanging on to your roots, and that's why Paul and Mark and I have gone to a lot of trouble to produce this album, *Liberal Traumas of the Sixties*. Well, as the song says, "Laugh and the world laughs with you." Well now, in the privacy of your own home you can laugh at all those assassinations again! It happened twenty years ago! What are you gonna do? Worry about it? That's right. We will also include five blank cassettes so that you can record the next major catastrophe yourself. Don't forget, there's fifty tabs of blotter acid on the back. Let's sing it!

hymn

Laugh
And the world laughs with you
Cry
And you cry alone
You know, bawling's a sin
Just bear it—and grin
Comedy's comfort, your birthright, your home

Hate
And the world will hate you
I'd rather take a punch line
Than a punch
Any day
You got to go for broke
Take the Jew with a joke
Why should I lie
We're all gonna die
Don't try to ask why
Just laugh your troubles away

god knows funny

If I had any brains at all, I would have devoted the time, energy, effort, and ingenuity into the creation of a new religion.

You heard me. Instead of squandering my time writing this book, I should have created an epistle of my own and then used my stand-up arena to convince the world that it was actually some sort of ancient text. It would have been the basis for a religion similar to the one I presented in the play you just read.

I could have claimed that I had discovered a series of cave drawings in the heart of, say, Tanzania, which were drawn by a shaman who used tickling as a cure-all. Here's how I see the whole thing in my head:

The drawings would have told the story of the shaman's tribe—known as the Hysterium—who, after discovering the joke, devoted their daily lives to perfecting it. They gleefully spent each day one-upping each other. The most elaborate of their jokes, however, sadly ended in the extinction of the tribe, thus the modern-day reference to a comic "killing."

It is unknown, I would tell my new followers, what that joke was, because, as legend has it, if one actually told it, the teller and all who heard it would die. But all was not lost because before they expired, the Hysterium developed every form of comedy that we know today. From slapstick to stand-up, the tribe members did it all in the name of the Father, the Sun, and the Holy Joke. They felt that this is what their Master of Ceremonies in the sky wanted from them. Humor was their form of worship, and laughter was the way in which they prayed. (My God, I'm a poetic fuck.)

So, besides the cave drawings, which featured many of their elaborate jokes—including that old chestnut of slipping on the bat shit into the tar pit (a true tribe favorite, as it was the subject of nearly two dozen drawings)—there is only one other reason we know of that the tribe existed. It was the sacred icon they left behind—the Funny Bone. Yes, the small bone that, when tapped on the ground, creates a vibration that causes involuntary laughter in anyone within earshot.

So that's it. An entirely new faith of my own design. I could have done it. Hell, I just did.

And imagine a religion where all God asks of you is to have a good laugh and then get back to trying to be a nice person. Let's face it, we could use something like this since we're living in a world that makes most of us so uptight that being nice is an exhausting proposition. Which is why my God would want each and every one of us to laugh—as it simply and miraculously alleviates stress.

What could offer more hope to the world than a religion based on laughter? And what sells better than false hope? Not a goddamn thing. I know. I've done extensive market research.

It's why when watching late-night television and the infomercials start telling you about a pill that promises to help you lose weight, or make your penis larger, or keep you young, your finger immediately itches to punch those digits that appear at the bottom of the screen. Even worse, there's the spectacularly well-advertised book *The Secret,* which is an incredible piece of bullshit, if you ask me. For those of you who missed it, the book actually tells you that you can have anything—and I mean fucking ANYTHING you want—merely if you allow yourself to think about it.

And, of course, not to be outdone by either of the examples above, there is every organized religion known to man.

So, I ask again, why not a religion based solely on the laugh? It would be a stroke of genius.

I figure, if God created us, how could he not have a really finely honed sense of humor? I think he definitely does. After all, he gave us a mind, which allows us to see life's incongruities and therefore enables us to laugh. As a matter of fact, I hold that laughter is one of the best arguments you can make to prove the existence of God—mine or anyone else's.

And just what is a laugh? While it is as mysterious as music, I see laughter as a cosmic hiccup that allows us to stare into the abyss while we straddle the grave. It makes a bad day bearable. It gives us the breathing room to deal with life's bullshit. It is the mechanism that enables us to cope with the deepest emotional pains and scars. And while sometimes it can be coaxed, laughter, by and large, is a completely uncontrollable physical reaction that seems to come out of nowhere. (If God truly did create Adam and Eve, imagine the moment after he finished his work when he realized what he had done—and the howling that would have followed as the tears rolled down his cheeks.)

Laughter truly is a gift from above, and without it we'd all be fucked. But like every other gift we receive in this life, it's not the *thing* that's so important, it's how we *use the thing.* In other words, what is it that inspires you to laugh? It varies from person to person, but luckily God, in his infinite wisdom, gave us a great starter kit.

To put it quite simply, the penis is funny on its own. The thing looks like a long-lost Marx brother and yet it is the instrument of reproduction. And let's fess up to the truth here: When it takes control of the brain—which is most of the time—it actually acts like a Marx brother. And that's when the fun explodes, so to speak.

Then there is the fart. You have to be brain-dead not to think a fart is funny. Sure, laughing at a run-of-the-mill bodily function is juvenile, but a brilliantly lit one—one that sparkles and flashes like a Fourth of July fireworks display—is a joy to behold and puts a smile on any young man's face.

And it's amazing how any major catastrophe fills e-mail boxes within hours with a cascade of jokes. We may want to—and, indeed, need to—weep, but the survival instinct also tells us to laugh.

So what it comes down to is this: I think that comedy and religion share a lot of similarities.

They both help people gather in a space to share a common vision.

They both give people a sense of transcendence.

They both offer hope.

They both offer comfort.

They both are mysteries.

And they both gather their biggest crowds on the weekends.

So, in conclusion, what can I tell you? You've heard it all before: Life's a bitch and then you die.

Hey, you know the rules, so you might as well enjoy it. Or bitch about it, as I do. It really doesn't matter one way or the other. Just do whatever helps get you through the day.

And worship anyone you want—be it Yahweh, Buddha, Jesus, a side order of fries, or a Weight Watchers meal.

The list is endless. Truly endless. But this book isn't.

So good-bye. And go with God, my children. Or go walk the dog.

talking to myself

Q: So what kind of response did *Me of Little Faith* provoke in people?

LB: Well, when I gave the book to my mother to read—critic No. 1—and said, "Okay, Mom, what do you think?" the first thing she said was, "Oh, you are in deep, deep trouble now. You are gonna get screwed." So I started to look at the book again and, I thought: "Oh, man. There could be problems. Because, you know, the Mormon stuff alone could make it tough for me to play Salt Lake again. And there's a pity. No jobs in Provo."

But I found that the only time there was any major flak at all was on the book tour. I was on *Talk of the Nation,* and this guy called up during the Q&A and he says: "Your comedy's really mean. You're mean. You're a mean-spirited person."

And I said, "Well, I don't really think so."

"Oh, yes, you are. And this book is, too."

And I said: "Well, can you give me specifics? Have you read the book?"

"No."

"Really, you haven't read the book? So I'm gonna have to sit here and talk to you about it?"

The problem when you're doing these kinds of interviews is that you have to maintain your sense of humor. But I got so angry. There are certain buzzwords—like *mean-spirited* or *vicious*—that just push a button in me, and I flip out. So I kind of went over the line and blew up. And then I said, "Well, you don't get it at all." I was kind of surprised that there wasn't more negative reaction to the book, but I'm really happy there wasn't more.

What was extraordinary was how many people read it—and I hate to say this, because out of context, this is the kind of thing that can destroy a career—for some sort of guidance. People seemed to read this book as if I were their . . . well, not Dr. Phil, but the guy who was kind of trying to find belief on his own. There's a billion religious books and spiritual guides out there. And some people kind of felt that while I wasn't a spiritual guide—let's not get creepy—I was on a journey that was parallel in some ways to theirs.

Q: You also made it okay not to have all the answers, and not to believe the dogma of organized religion.

LB: Yeah. And people found that comforting, which was fascinating to me, because it was so unexpected. I expected more of a reaction like, "What is the matter with you?"

The chapter that is pivotal for people who really liked the

book is the chapter about my brother and his death. Because people really can relate to that. And I don't think they expected me to share that kind of experience with them.

Q: It also points out that there are a lot of different spiritual realities.

LB: I wrote a chapter in the book about a woman I knew when I was a kid. We were in school together. I've never seen her since, but she wrote to me out of the blue telling me that I was her son's favorite comic and that I'd never meet the Lord if I continued to use profanity and take the Lord's name in vain. So I wrote a chapter about her and her letter, and I thought I might hear from her. But I never did. Which surprised me, because I've been back in the Washington area, where she still lives.

But the amazing thing to me was that her letter arrived literally at the point in my writing where I'm thinking to myself, "Oh, man, what am I gonna write next?" And this letter shows up, and she goes off on the language I use, the way I see things, and my lack of faith. I'll be frying in hell for eternity. But she'll be praying for me, in hopes that someday we meet in heaven again. Whoo! You know, it'd be like being on the cafeteria line again in high school. Really? The milk's still two cents?

What's funny about all this is that she's writing to me about my lack of faith. And yet the universe sends her to show up at my door with this letter, so I got my next chapter.

Q: What did you learn about the process of writing with this book?

LB: The thing I would say to everyone who writes a book is that you just have to get it done. But there were times when I reread the finished book and realized that there are some details I forgot. Not so much punchlines—I mean, occasionally I think about punchlines—but mostly I remembered things I could have added if I'd remembered.

The major lesson I learned from writing this book, more than anything else, is that you just write. ("That's brilliant, Lewis. Really? You write?" Yeah.) For years when I wrote plays and I wrote my first book, I thought that the way you write something is that you have to have a full thought and then you write it down. That's not true. It's great to have that. If you have that, you have a sense of what you're doing. But if you don't have that kind of direction, then you have to just sit down and start writing about what you're thinking about. And the way you find out what you're writing about is to write. So you just start writing.

And that's hard, I think. It certainly was hard for me, because it took over thirty years—forty plays and a book—for me to get to the point where I realized that. You just have to sit down and write—badly, whether you like it or not—and realize that no one is gonna look at it. And if you can turn off the critic in your head that says to you: "You're a moron. This is so stupid. I can't believe they're paying you for this shit!" you can get something done. Eventually

I wrote whatever came to my mind. And 90 percent of the time, it led to something.

What I had been doing when I was writing is say to myself, "I can't really think of something. I'm gonna go lie down, and then I'm gonna have a revelation." And generally it would go, "I'll lie down and I'll try to think of something. Well, let's masturbate. Nap." I would love to see a poll of people who've written books, and really, what the percentage of masturbation is in their lives while they're writing. Because it must be huge.

Q: Talk about the reasons you included *The Laundry Hour* in the book.

LB: Here's what's interesting about *The Laundry Hour.* No one has written to me about that play in a positive way. People say, "You put that play in," like I was screwing people. "You son of a bitch, you made me read a *play.*" And it was totally dismissed by a certain group of people. (What's sad is that this is proof that I'm actually reading my MySpace commentaries and the comments section on Amazon.com.) As you read them, you realize that this is proof you're a moron. Because you're reading a comment from some person you don't even know and you read it as if you're reading a commentary from George Bernard Shaw, who had to come back from the dead to tell you what a piece of shit you are.

And what's sicker is then you see the link that says, "See

some of my other criticism." And you go—"Yeah, let's see what else he's written." And you find out that your critic didn't like some kind of sci-fi trilogy you've never heard of. You know, *The Gorgon Continues*. And you go, "Holy God. Well, no wonder he didn't like the play."

I think what I really learned is that people have an aversion to reading plays. I don't understand it. I got into playwriting in part because one of the great things about it is that you don't have to describe anything. When you're writing a story you think, "I've got to describe the sun? Every fucking person can see it. What do I gotta tell 'em?" So once you realize you're not an adjective or adverb repository, you can focus on conversation.

You know, I'm fascinated by the way people talk. And that was the reason I wrote dialogue. I realized I loved reading plays more than fiction. Because there's no description. There's nothing to follow. You don't have to track a paragraph. You can write "the door opens" instead of "The big bronze door, which appeared so imposing, like his father's judging of him" or whatever. You don't have to do that.

Q: Since *Me of Little Faith* was first published, are people laughing at different things now than they did before?

LB: I hope so. I think our sense of humor is always evolving, but I could be wrong on that. I do know it's my job to find different things for us to laugh at. When I started talking about Obama, the topic was hope. I initially started by just saying, "If you're a kid, there's nothing better than hope. But at my age, who could give a shit? You know, the hope train's passed me by." And people really laughed at that. And I said, "You know, if I could only sing a blues song now and close the show, it'd be perfect."

Q: Are different things irritating you now, or causing you to think that the world is a different place from what it was when you started to write the book?

LB: Oh, yeah. It's like we woke up from an eight-year frat party and now we've got to clean the bong water out of the rug and throw away all the plastic cups and take the kegs back to the liquor stores.

People keep asking, "Well, is Obama gonna make a difference in your comedy? Do you think it's gonna be tougher?" The thing is, you're a comic. It's not like I rely on presidents of the United States to write my material. It's just the luck of the draw that we had eight years with a guy who, if you paid any attention as a comedian, was a windfall.

In a sense, I don't think much has changed. Because the stuff I talk about in terms of these guys was not the headlines. It was trying to go behind what was going on. And people ask, "What will you say about Obama?" I don't know. But I do know that there'll be some jackass running around. I mean, Bush begot Cheney, who begot Condoleezza Rice. There was Colin Powell at the UN showing you pictures of things that don't even have anything to do with weapons of mass destruction. You have to say: "You think the bad stuff is over? We trash Iraq, we just make a complete mess of all of our alliances, and then you say, 'Look, we elected a black guy.' Wow! So that makes up for everything?"

It's like if you go back to the Tate-LaBianca murders, Charlie Manson's Helter Skelter. He kills everybody, and there's blood everywhere in the house, and it's disgusting. And let's say he buries the bodies outside and then goes back in and completely renovates the house. And you go, "Oh, well, he's innocent."

The reason I think most things don't change is that if stupidity were oil, we'd be the richest country on the planet.

ACKNOWLEDGMENTS

I would like to thank: My editors. Hank Gallo, who went beyond the call of duty and is a gifted writer in his own right. He should get more credit than I am going to give him. Jake Morrissey, who kept me from suicidal inclinations when all seemed hopeless and whose faith in my writing saw me through to the end of this book. Maybe he wasn't so much an editor as a priest.

My producer. Joseph Papp, who let us develop *The Laundry Hour* at the New York Shakespeare Festival. And my collaborators. Mark Linn-Baker. Bill Peters. Paul Schierhorn.

My friends who let me write about them and gave me input. Cliff Figallo. James Yoshimura. Michael Bodine.

My friend Kosh, who asked to design the book jacket—a lovely gesture from a genius.

My friend and tour driver Frank Moreno. Never have I felt safer in any form of transportation. He drove me across country three times during the course of the writing of this book and had to listen as I screamed at the computer and the heavens.

All those who had to live through the pain. Joanne Astrow. Mark Lonow. Shannon Kennedy. Ben Brewer. Jeff Costa. John Bowman. Shannon Marie Kerr. Jim Gosnell. Steve Fisher. Betsy Boyd, Martha Harrell. Steve Olsen and the West Bank Café. And all my friends who had to put up with my whining.

And all those who serve in our military, for always going way beyond the call of duty, especially lately, so I could write a book like this.